stitching
for the seasons

20 Quilt Projects

Combine Patchwork, Embroidery & Wool Appliqué

Jen Daly

C&T PUBLISHING

Text copyright © 2019 by Jen Daly

Photography and artwork copyright © 2019 by C&T Publishing, Inc.

Publisher: Amy Marson

Creative Director: Gailen Runge

Acquisitions Editor: Roxane Cerda

Managing Editor: Liz Aneloski

Editors: Liz Aneloski and Beth Baumgartel

Technical Editor: Linda Johnson

Cover/Book Designer: April Mostek

Production Coordinator: Tim Manibusan

Production Editor: Jennifer Warren

Illustrators: Mary E. Flynn and Linda Johnson

Photo Assistants: Mai Yong Vang and Rachel Holmes

Style and instructional photography by Kelly Burgoyne and flat shots by Mai Yong Vang of C&T Publishing, Inc., unless otherwise noted

Published by C&T Publishing, Inc., P.O. Box 1456, Lafayette, CA 94549

Library of Congress Cataloging-in-Publication Data

Names: Daly, Jen, 1970-

Title: Stitching for the seasons : 20 quilt projects combine patchwork, embroidery & wool appliqué / Jen Daly.

Description: Lafayette, CA : C&T Publishing, Inc., 2019.

Identifiers: LCCN 2018015932 | ISBN 9781617456718 (soft cover)

Subjects: LCSH: Patchwork--Patterns. | Quilting--Patterns.

Classification: LCC TT835 .D345 2019 | DDC 746.46/041--dc23

LC record available at https://lccn.loc.gov/2018015932

Printed in China

10 9 8 7 6 5 4 3 2 1

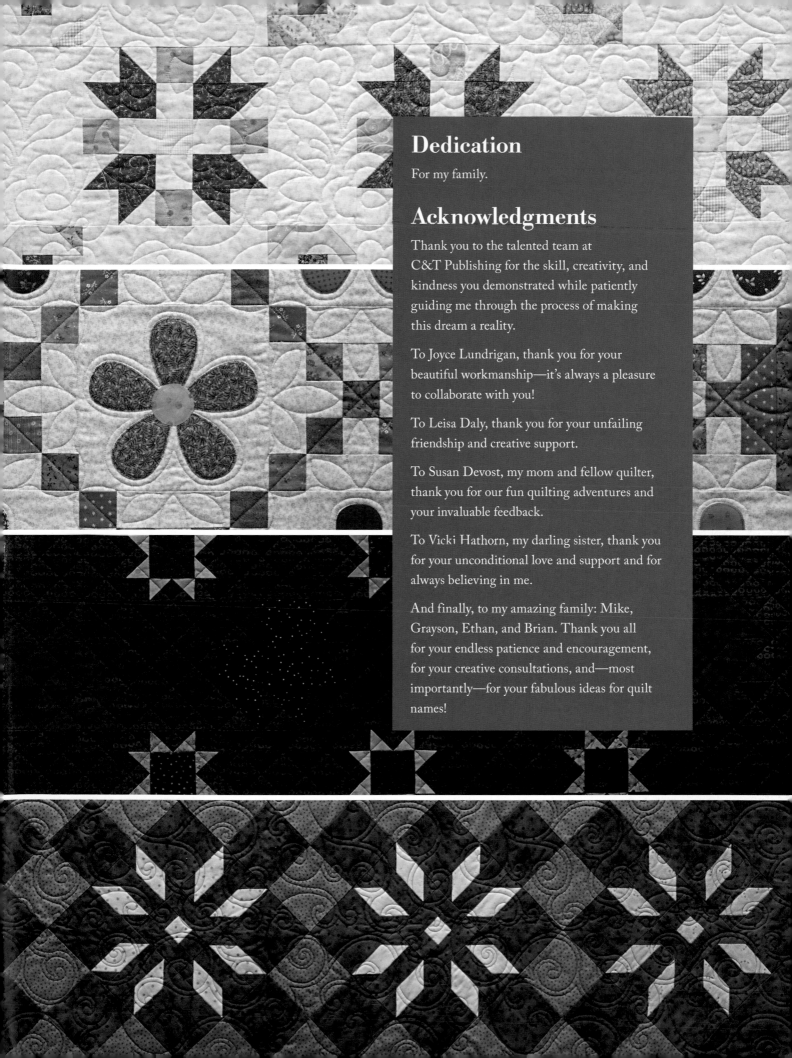

Dedication

For my family.

Acknowledgments

Thank you to the talented team at C&T Publishing for the skill, creativity, and kindness you demonstrated while patiently guiding me through the process of making this dream a reality.

To Joyce Lundrigan, thank you for your beautiful workmanship—it's always a pleasure to collaborate with you!

To Leisa Daly, thank you for your unfailing friendship and creative support.

To Susan Devost, my mom and fellow quilter, thank you for our fun quilting adventures and your invaluable feedback.

To Vicki Hathorn, my darling sister, thank you for your unconditional love and support and for always believing in me.

And finally, to my amazing family: Mike, Grayson, Ethan, and Brian. Thank you all for your endless patience and encouragement, for your creative consultations, and—most importantly—for your fabulous ideas for quilt names!

contents

fall 53

   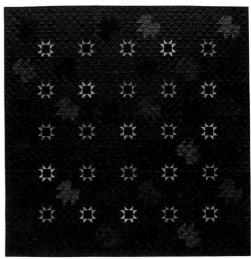

winter 77

introduction

I've lived most of my life in New England, and one of the best parts about living in this corner of the world is the changing of the seasons. In New England, the four seasons are very distinct, each with its own look and its own flavor. Spring is fresh and invigorating—quietly colorful with its shades of pink, yellow, and (my favorite) chartreuse. Summer is fast-paced and festive, with brilliant color everywhere you look. Fall is simply gorgeous—all reds, rusts, oranges, and golds set against a backdrop of impossibly blue skies. And winter's restful atmosphere is reflected in its monochromatic palette of white, grays, and blues. Each season is different, but they are all wonderful, and one of my favorite ways to celebrate the changing seasons is with quilts.

For me, quilts are not just functional objects; they are art. Quilts connect us to the past, express an idea or evoke emotions, and are just so pretty to look at! In my home, I have quilts everywhere—they're draped over railings and armchairs, hanging on walls and from door knobs, resting on benches as pillows, and covering tables and beds. Quilts make my home warm and inviting, and as the seasons change, I love to pack away the past season's quilts and pull out the new. Every year, it's like welcoming back old friends, and it reminds me to take a moment to savor the season I'm in.

In this book, you'll find twenty projects to help you commemorate the seasons and decorate your home. For each season, I've designed a pillow, a mini quilt, a table runner, a lap quilt, and a charming Little House wallhanging. You can display the quilts in the same spots in your home—rotating them as the seasons pass—or scatter them about and leave them out year-round.

The projects in this book vary in size and complexity and combine many different techniques and materials. My "everything but the kitchen sink" approach to quilting evolved because I love it all—big, cozy lap quilts and the charm of quilting in miniature; the speed of machine piecing and the Zen of handwork; cottons and wools, fibers and buttons—and when I started to mix and match, I fell in love with the warm, homespun result.

To that end, in addition to traditional piecing, you'll be using paper piecing, raw-edge and dimensional appliqué, wool appliqué, and simple embroidery to make scrappy, richly textured quilts with a touch of whimsy. I hope that you'll be inspired to try these techniques to personalize your quilts and that you'll change them up to suit your taste. These are your projects, for your home and your unique experience of the seasons. Now let's get started!

—Jen

spring

After a long New England winter, spring is sublime! The soft air begins to warm, songbirds return home, and gentle rains encourage the growth of bright chartreuse-green leaves and delicate flowers. Everything seems fresh and clean, and it is such a relief to finally throw open the windows and leave the house without a coat!

little house—spring wallhanging

Spring is underway at Little House. A gentle rain is falling, green leaves are budding, and pink and yellow flowers are just beginning to bloom.

This sweet little wallhanging incorporates some of my favorite techniques in one tidy little package— miniature patchwork, a bit of wool appliqué, simple stitching, and a darling bird button.

Materials

Cotton yardage is based on 40˝-wide fabric. Wool sizes are for felted wool. This pattern is scrap or precut friendly, though an entire precut pack or roll is not *required. Precut sizes shown in the materials list indicate scrap sizes as well.*

FABRICS

Light blue print: 1 precut 10˝ square for appliqué background

Blue-green prints: ⅛ yard for single-fold binding

4 assorted precut 2½˝ strips at least 9˝ long for quilt-center borders

12 assorted mini charm squares 2½˝ × 2½˝ for Flying Geese backgrounds and bottom row sashing

4 assorted charm squares 5˝ × 5˝ for tulip and Square-in-a-Square background

Pink prints: 5 assorted mini charm squares 2½˝ × 2½˝ for top row blocks

Yellow prints: 4 assorted mini charm squares 2½˝ × 2½˝ for Flying Geese blocks

Backing: 1 fat quarter *or* 1 rectangle 12˝ × 16˝

FELTED WOOL

Green: 2˝ × 7˝ for grass

Dark red: 3˝ × 5˝ for house

Textured dark brown: 2˝ × 4˝ for roof

Medium brown: 2˝ × 4˝ for tree

Dark brown: 2˝ × 2˝ for windows

Dark gold: 2˝ × 2˝ for door and chimney

White: 2˝ × 2˝ for cloud

Light brown: Scrap for rabbit

Blue: Scrap for birdhouse

EMBROIDERY FLOSS

Colors to match wool

Pink and yellow for flowers

Blue for raindrops

OTHER SUPPLIES

Batting: 12˝ × 16˝

Lightweight paper-backed fusible web (17˝ wide): ¼ yard

Foundation paper for paper piecing

Small bird button (I used the Tiny Sweet Heart Bird [1192.T] from Just Another Button Company.)

Water-soluble fabric marking pen

Cutting

LIGHT BLUE PRINT

- Cut 1 square 8″ × 8″ for the appliqué center.

BLUE-GREEN PRINTS

From yardage, cut:

- 2 strips 1¼″ × width of fabric (WOF) for the binding

From 4 assorted precut 2½″ strips, cut the quilt-center borders:

- 2 strips 1¼″ × 8″
- 2 strips 1¼″ × 6½″

From 12 assorted mini charm squares, cut:

- 4 rectangles 1¼″ × 2½″ for the bottom row sashing
- 8 squares 2¼″ × 2¼″, each cut in half diagonally once to make 8 triangle *pairs* (B)

From each of the 4 assorted charm squares, cut 1 set of:

- 2 squares 2¼″ × 2¼″, each cut in half diagonally once to make 4 matching print triangles (D)

PINK PRINTS

From each of 3 assorted charm squares, cut 1 set of:

- 1 square 1½″ × 1½″ (E)
- 1 square 2″ × 2″ (F)
- 1 rectangle 2″ × 3″ (G)

From 5 assorted mini charm squares, cut:

- 4 rectangles 1½″ × 2½″ (A)
- 1 square 1¾″ × 1¾″ (C)

YELLOW PRINTS

From 4 assorted mini charm squares, cut:

- 4 rectangles 1½″ × 2½″ (A)

The Quilt Center

Because of the narrow branches and the small pieces, the fusible web method for wool appliqué is most suitable. Refer to Fusible Web Method (page 109) for step-by-step instructions. Refer to Stitching Wool Appliqués (page 109) as needed.

APPLIQUÉ

1. Use the general Little House Wallhanging appliqué patterns (page 13) for the house, roof, windows, door, chimney, tree, and grass, and the Little House—Spring Wallhanging appliqué patterns (page 14) for the cloud, rabbit, and birdhouse to prepare the wool appliqués.

2. In the center of the light blue fabric, draw a 6½″ × 6½″ square with a water-soluble marking pen. This square is the appliqué placement area, *including* the ¼″ seam allowance, and will be the trim size after the appliqué and embroidery have been completed. (The finished size will measure 6″ × 6″.)

3. Use the project photo as a guide to position the wool appliqués within the drawn square. Make sure that the house is centered from left to right and that the grass will be enclosed within the seams of the finished project.

Note: Certain appliqué pieces overlap, so be sure to tuck the bottom layer of pieces under the top layers before fusing. For example, the grass overlaps the bottom edges of the house and door.

4. Once you are satisfied with the placement of the wool appliqués, fuse the pieces to the background.

5. Whipstitch the wool appliqués in place using *1 strand* of embroidery floss. Use *gold* floss for the house and windows and *dark brown* floss for the door. For the remaining appliqués, match the floss to the wool. It isn't necessary to whipstitch the bottom and side edges of the grass because they'll be enclosed within the seams of the finished project.

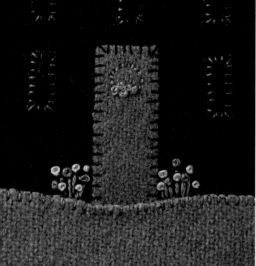

EMBROIDERY

Refer to Embroidery Basics (page 110) for detailed information. Use *2 strands* of floss for all embroidery unless otherwise indicated.

1. Trace the dashed lines of the tree branches (see the Little House Wallhanging appliqué patterns, page 13) onto the fabric using the water-soluble fabric marking pen.

2. Backstitch the tree branches using *medium brown* floss.

3. Use *green* floss to stitch the following: French knots for the buds along the tree branches and a single straight stitch (one each) for the flower stems on either side of the door, the tree, and the rabbit. Take tiny backstitches to embroider the wreath on the door.

4. Alternate *pink and yellow* floss to stitch French knots for the flowers on either side of the door, the tree, and the rabbit, and on the bottom of the wreath.

5. Use *light brown* floss to stitch long straight stitches along the upper angled edges of the birdhouse to make the roof. Repeat long straight stitches as necessary to give the roof enough thickness. Stitch a French knot for the birdhouse opening with the same *light brown* floss.

6. Use *blue* floss to stitch single lazy daisy loops for the raindrops beneath the cloud.

TRIMMING

Trim the appliquéd and embroidered quilt center to 6½˝ × 6½˝ along the marked lines you drew on the fabric previously.

Making the Paper-Pieced Blocks

Note: Foundation Paper-Piecing Patterns

The foundation paper-piecing patterns are available to photocopy from the book or to download and print at **tinyurl.com/11308-patterns-download.**

Copy the Little House Wallhanging top row foundation patterns (page 12) and Little House—Spring Wallhanging bottom row foundation patterns (page 14) onto foundation paper. Cut out each pattern ¼˝ beyond its outer dashed line. Refer to Paper-Piecing Basics (page 105) for step-by-step instructions.

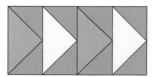

A. Flying Geese unit   **B.** Square-in-a-Square

TOP ROW BLOCKS

1. Paper piece 2 Flying Geese units *(fig. A)*, covering the areas in numerical order. Use the pieces designated for each area as follows:

Areas 1 and 7: Pink rectangles (A)

Areas 2 and 3, 5 and 6, 8 and 9, 11 and 12: Blue-green triangle pairs (B)

Areas 4 and 10: Yellow rectangles (A)

2. Paper piece 1 Square-in-a-Square block *(fig. B)*, covering the areas in numerical order. Use the pieces designated for each area as follows:

Area 1: Pink square (C)

Areas 2, 3, 4, and 5: 1 set of 4 matching blue-green triangles (D)

BOTTOM ROW BLOCKS

1. Paper piece a Tulip block, covering the areas in numerical order. When working on a block, choose 1 pink set for E, F, and G. Use the pieces designated for each area as follows:

Area 1: Pink square (E)

Areas 2 and 3, 6 and 7: 1 set of 4 matching blue-green triangles (D)

Area 4: Pink square (F)

Area 5: Pink rectangle (G)

2. Make 3. *fig. C*

C. Tulip block

Assembling the Quilt

Use a ¼″ seam allowance. Follow the pressing arrows provided in the diagram(s). For more information about pressing seam allowances, see Pressing Matters (page 19).

1. Sew the 2 blue-green 6½″ quilt-center border strips to the right and left sides of the trimmed quilt center.

2. Sew the 2 remaining blue-green quilt-center border strips to the top and bottom to finish the framed quilt center.

3. Lay out 2 Flying Geese units and position the Square-in-a-Square block between them. The Flying Geese should point toward the center. Join the pieces. Gently remove the paper from behind the blocks, and press the seam allowances open to complete the top row.

4. Lay out 4 blue-green bottom-row sashing rectangles and 3 Tulip blocks in alternating positions. Join the pieces. Gently remove the paper from behind the Tulip blocks to complete the bottom row.

5. Lay out the top row, framed quilt center, and bottom row as shown. Join the rows and quilt center.

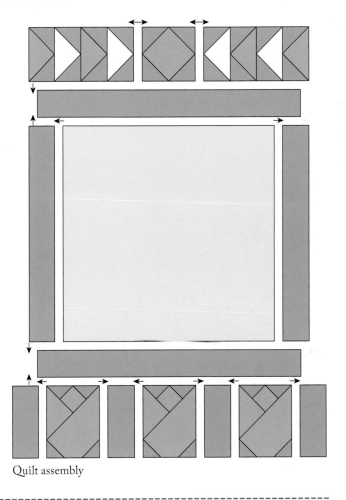

Quilt assembly

Finishing the Quilt

1. Referring to the project photo, stitch the small bird button to the roof of the house.

2. Layer the quilt top, batting, and backing. If desired, baste and quilt the layers. (Because of the small size of the project, quilting is not necessary.)

3. If desired, prepare and stitch a hanging sleeve to the back of the quilt. Refer to Adding a Hanging Sleeve to a Small Quilt (page 104) for step-by-step instructions.

4. Bind the quilt. Refer to Single-Fold Binding (page 104) for step-by-step binding instructions.

little house wallhanging

Top Row Foundation Patterns

Photocopy this page once onto foundation paper.

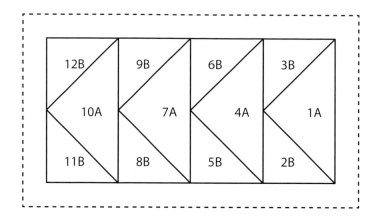

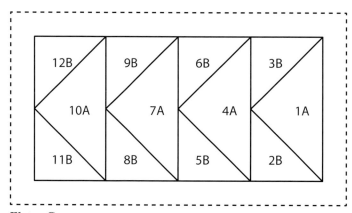

Flying Geese

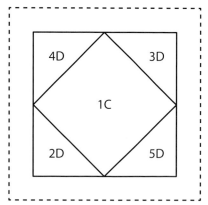

Square-in-a-Square

Appliqué Patterns

Patterns are reversed for fusible web appliqué. Cut 1 of each except where noted.

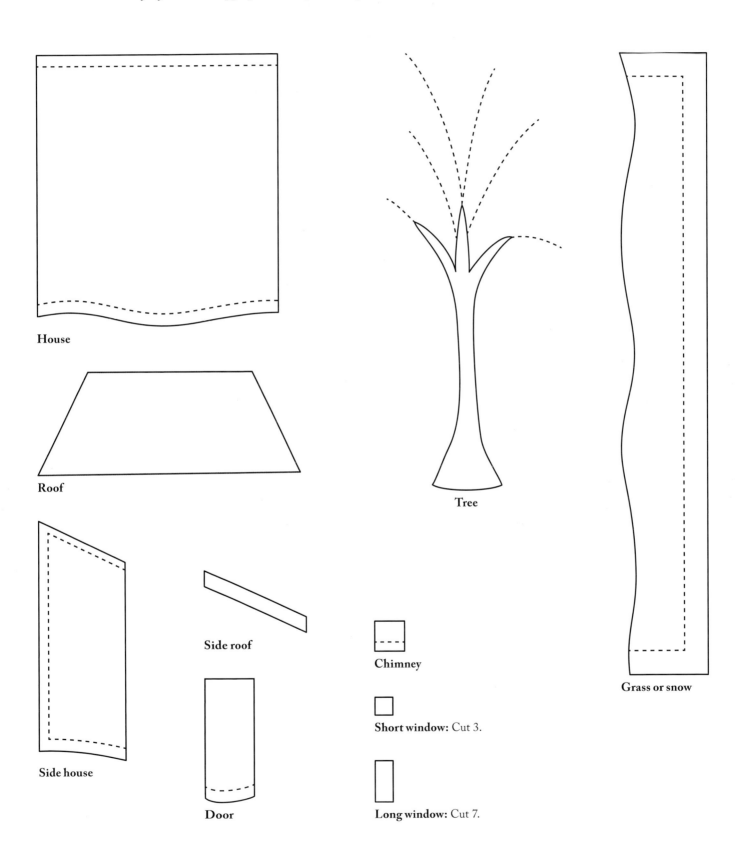

House

Roof

Tree

Side roof

Side house

Chimney

Door

Short window: Cut 3.

Long window: Cut 7.

Grass or snow

little house—spring wallhanging

Bottom Row Foundation Patterns

Photocopy this page once onto foundation paper.

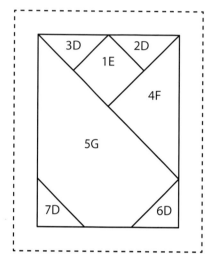
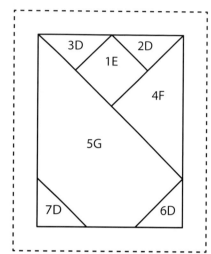
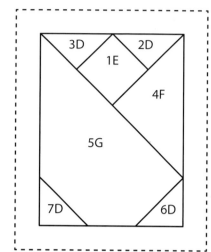

Tulips

Appliqué Patterns

Patterns are reversed for fusible web appliqué. Cut 1 of each.

Cloud

Rabbit

Birdhouse

think spring pillow

Announce the arrival of spring with this charming little pillow, featuring a simple wool appliqué bird perched atop a leafy branch. Make this fast and fun project with a mini charm pack of your favorite spring fabrics.

Materials

Cotton yardage is based on 40˝-wide fabric. Wool sizes are for felted wool.

FABRICS

Assorted spring prints: 1 mini charm square pack *or* 42 squares 2½˝ × 2½˝ (I used La Belle Fleur by French General.)

Medium-blue textured solid: ½ yard for pillow backing and pillow inset

Lining fabric: ½ yard of muslin

FELTED WOOL

White: 3˝ × 5˝ for bird

Medium brown: 2˝ × 6˝ for branch

Medium blue: 2˝ × 2˝ for wing

Green: 2˝ × 2˝ for leaves

EMBROIDERY FLOSS

Colors to match wool

White perle cotton #8 for bird

OTHER SUPPLIES

Batting: 16˝ × 20˝

Pillow form: 12˝ × 16˝

Lightweight paper-backed fusible web: 7˝ × 7˝

Water-soluble fabric marking pen

Cutting

ASSORTED SPRING PRINTS

- Cut 42 squares 2½″ × 2½″ if you've chosen not to use a mini charm square pack.

MEDIUM-BLUE TEXTURED SOLID

- Cut 1 rectangle 5″ × 7″.
- Cut 2 backing panels 12″ × 12½″.

LINING FABRIC

- Cut 1 rectangle 16″ × 20″.

Making the Pillow Top

Use a ¼″ seam allowance. Follow the pressing arrows provided in the diagram(s).
For more information about pressing seam allowances, see Pressing Matters (page 19).

PILLOW INSET APPLIQUÉ

Because of the narrow branch and the sharp point of the bird's beak, the fusible web method for wool appliqué is best for this project. Refer to Fusible Web Method (page 109) for step-by-step instructions. Refer to Stitching Wool Appliqués (page 109) as needed.

1. Use the Think Spring Pillow appliqué patterns (next page) to prepare the wool appliqués.

2. With a water-soluble marking pen, draw a 4½″ × 6½″ rectangle centered on the medium blue rectangle. This rectangle is the appliqué placement area, *including* the ¼″ seam allowance, and will be the trim size after the appliqué has been completed. (The finished size will measure 4″ × 6″.)

3. Use the project photo close-up as a guide to position the wool appliqués within the drawn rectangle. Make sure that the leaves overlap the tips of the branches and that the right edge of the branch rests on the drawn line of the rectangle. This way it will be enclosed within the seam of the finished project. Once you are satisfied with the placement of the wool appliqués, fuse the pieces to the background.

4. Blanket stitch the bird appliqué in place with *white perle cotton #8*.

5. Whipstitch the remaining pieces in place using *1 strand* of embroidery floss that matches the wool.

6. Trim the pillow inset to 4½″ × 6½″ using the lines you marked in Step 2.

PILLOW TOP ASSEMBLY

1. Lay out the appliquéd pillow inset and the 42 squares as shown.

2. When you are happy with the arrangement, join the squares into rows; then join the rows.

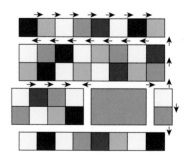

Pillow top assembly

EMBROIDERY

Refer to Embroidery Basics (page 110) for detailed information. Use *2 strands* of floss for all embroidery.

1. Use the Think Spring Pillow embroidery pattern (below) to mark the lettering on the pillow inset with the water-soluble fabric marking pen. A lightbox or other light source is helpful.

2. Layer the pillow top, batting, and lining fabric. Baste.

3. Backstitch the lettering on the pillow inset through all layers using *white* floss.

4. Stitch a French knot for the bird's eye using *brown* floss.

QUILTING

1. Quilt the pillow top as desired. The featured pillow was machine quilted ¼˝ along both sides of each seam, stopping or starting at the inset as necessary and knotting the thread ends at the back (lining side) of the pillow top.

2. Trim the batting and lining even with the pillow top.

Finishing the Pillow

1. To make the pillow back, hem one of the 12½˝ edges of each backing panel. To do this, fold the edge toward the wrong side ⅜˝ and then ⅜˝ again, and press.

2. Stitch close to the inside folded edge.

3. Layer one backing panel on the pillow top, right sides together and raw edges aligned.

4. Layer the remaining panel on the opposite side of the pillow top, right sides together and raw edges aligned. Pin.

5. Stitch around all the edges and through all the layers with a ¼˝ seam.

6. Trim the corners to reduce bulk, turn the pillow right side out, and insert the pillow form.

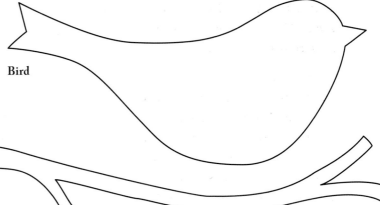

Pillow assembly

---

think spring pillow

Appliqué Patterns

Patterns are reversed for fusible web appliqué.
Cut 1 of each except where noted.

Leaf: Cut 3.

Wing

Branch

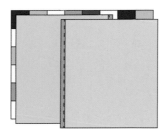

Bird

Embroidery Pattern

Pillow lettering

tickled pink mini quilt

Pair pretty pinks with warm white and bright green for the perfect spring palette. Simple embroidered flowers and a plaid binding add a touch of whimsy to this sweet little quilt.

Materials

Cotton yardage is based on 40˝-wide fabric. This pattern is scrap or precut friendly, though an entire precut pack or roll is not required. Precut sizes shown in the materials list indicate scrap sizes as well.

FABRICS

Cream print: ⅓ yard for background, sashing, and borders

Pink-and-green plaid: ¼ yard for binding

Pink prints: 4 assorted precut 10˝ squares *or* 4 assorted charm squares* 5˝ × 5˝ for flowers

Green print: 1 precut 10˝ square for narrow sashing

Yellow print: 1 charm square 5˝ × 5˝ for flower centers

Dark pink print: 1 charm square 5˝ × 5˝ for cornerstones

Backing: 1 fat quarter

EMBROIDERY FLOSS

Yellow

Green

Pink: 3 or 4 shades

OTHER SUPPLIES

Batting: 18˝ × 18˝

Water-soluble fabric marking pen

Cream quilting thread

Cutting must be exact when using charm squares!

Cutting

CREAM PRINT

- Cut 2 strips 2¼″ × width of fabric (WOF). Crosscut into:

  2 strips 2¼″ × 14½″ for the border

  2 strips 2¼″ × 11″ for the border

- Cut 1 strip 2″ × WOF. Crosscut into:

  8 squares 2″ × 2″ for the small petals

  16 squares 1″ × 1″ for the flower centers

- Cut 2 strips 1½″ × WOF. Crosscut into:

  17 squares 1½″ × 1½″ for the large petals and center cornerstone

  16 rectangles 1½″ × 1″ for the flower centers

  8 rectangles 1½″ × 1¼″ for the narrow sashing ends

  8 rectangles 1½″ × 2½″ for the sashing

PINK-AND-GREEN PLAID

- Cut 2 strips 2¼″ × WOF for the binding.

PINK PRINTS

From each precut 10″ square or charm square, cut 1 set of:

- 4 rectangles 2½″ × 1½″ for the large petals

- 2 squares 2″ × 2″ for the small petals

GREEN PRINT

From 1 precut 10″ square, cut:

- 8 rectangles 1¼″ × 1½″ for the narrow sashing ends

- 4 strips 1¼″ × 5½″ for the narrow sashing

YELLOW PRINT

- Cut 16 squares 1″ × 1″ for the flower centers.

DARK PINK PRINT

- Cut 4 squares 1¼″ × 1¼″ for the narrow sashing cornerstones.

Note: Pressing Matters

Pressing arrows are provided in the instructional diagrams and are important for a flat, professional finish. Press after sewing each seam. Generally speaking, seams are pressed toward the darker fabrics and pieced seams are pressed toward unpieced areas such as sashings or borders. Occasionally seams may be pressed open where too much bulk occurs.

Making the Quarter-Flower Units

Use a ¼″ seam allowance. Follow the pressing arrows provided in the diagram(s). For more information about pressing seam allowances, see Pressing Matters (above right).

FLOWER PETALS

1. On the wrong side of 8 cream 2″ squares, use a pencil to lightly draw a diagonal line from corner to corner.

2. Layer a marked cream square atop a 2″ pink square, right sides together. Sew a scant ¼″ from each side of the drawn line. *fig. A*

3. Cut the unit apart on the drawn line to make 2 half-square triangles; press open. Trim to measure 1½″ × 1½″ to use as small petals.

4. Repeat to make 16 small petals, 4 from each pink print. *fig. B*

5. Use a pencil to lightly draw a diagonal line from corner to corner

on the wrong side of 16 cream 1½″ squares. Set aside the remaining 1½″ cream square for the quilt's center cornerstone.

6. Layer a marked cream square onto one end of a pink rectangle, right sides together. Stitch the pair together on the drawn line. Be mindful of the stitching line's orientation! *fig. C*

7. Trim the seam allowance to ¼″.

8. Repeat with the remaining marked cream squares and pink rectangles to make a total of 16 large petals, 4 from each pink print. Keep small and large petals of the same print together. *fig. D*

A.

B. Small petal

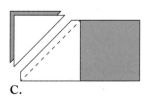

C.

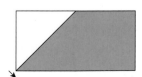

D. Large petal

FLOWER CENTER

1. Sew a 1″ cream square to a 1″ yellow square. Make 16.

2. Sew a cream rectangle 1½″ × 1″ to the top of the cream-and-yellow unit as shown. Repeat to make 16 flower centers. *fig. E*

E. Flower center

ASSEMBLY

1. Join a flower center to the top of each small petal. Take note of how the blocks are oriented. *fig. F*

2. Sew the large petals to the right side of the small petal / flower center units. Note that the pink prints of the small and large petals should match.

3. Repeat to make 4 matching quarter-flower units of each pink print. *fig. G*

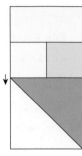

F.

Assembling the Quilt

At this point, decide which flower print you want in which corner. Refer to the quilt center assembly diagram (next page) often to orient and place the blocks throughout construction.

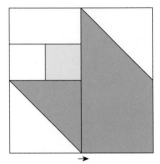

G. Quarter-flower unit

QUILT CENTER ROW

1. Select 4 quarter-flower units, one of each print. Arrange these in a square so that the flower centers all point toward the center.

2. Sew a cream sashing rectangle between the 2 top blocks and another between the 2 bottom blocks to make 2 separate rows.

3. Make a center sashing row by sewing the cream center cornerstone (previously set aside) between 2 cream sashing rectangles.

4. Use the center sashing row to join the top and bottom flower rows created in Step 2. *fig. H*

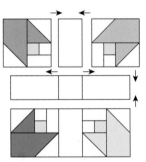

H. Quilt center

> ### *tip*
> To help keep your work square, make a small pencil mark within the seam allowance at the centers of the long sides of the narrow green sashing strips and the short sides of the intersecting cream sashing rectangles. Align these marks before pinning and sewing.

5. Sew a green narrow sashing strip to the left and right sides of the quilt center.

6. Select 4 more quarter-flower units, one of each print. Arrange these to the left and right sides of the quilt center, setting prints across from their matching prints. Their flower centers will all point outward.

7. On each side, join the top and bottom quarter-flower units by adding a cream sashing rectangle between them.

8. Join the side flower units to the green narrow sashing on each side to complete the quilt center row. *fig. I*

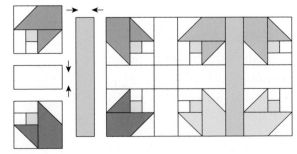

I. Quilt center row

NARROW SASHING

1. Join a cream narrow sashing rectangle to a green narrow sashing rectangle (both measure 1½″ × 1¼″) along their short sides to make a narrow sashing end unit. Repeat for a total of 8 narrow sashing end units. *fig. J*

J. Narrow sashing end unit

2. Sew a dark pink cornerstone square to both ends of the remaining 2 green narrow sashing strips.

3. Join the green side of a narrow sashing end unit to each dark pink cornerstone. Set the 2 narrow sashing rows aside. *fig. K*

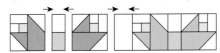

K. Narrow sashing row

TOP AND BOTTOM ROWS

1. Sew a narrow sashing end unit between 2 quarter-flower units of the same print. Both flower centers should point up and away from each other. The green print should sit between the pink print of the large petals. Make 4 same-print half-flower units.

2. For the top row, select the 2 half-flower units that match the prints at the top of the quilt center row. Orient the half-flower units so that they face upward. Join them together with a cream sashing rectangle between them.

3. Repeat Step 2 with the remaining 2 half-flower units and the last cream sashing rectangle to make the bottom row. Make sure the half-flower units face downward and the prints are on the correct side. *fig. L*

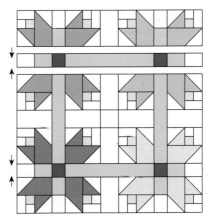

L. Top row (Bottom row is a mirror image in different prints.)

ASSEMBLY

1. Referring to the quilt center assembly diagram (at right), lay out the top, center, and bottom rows with a narrow sashing row between each.

2. Join the narrow sashing rows to the top and bottom of the quilt center row.

3. Join the top and bottom rows to the narrow sashing rows. At this point, the quilt should measure 11″ × 11″. *fig. M*

4. Sew an 11″ cream border strip to the left and right sides of the quilt center.

5. Sew a 14½″ cream border strip to the top and bottom of the quilt center. *fig. N*

M. Quilt center assembly

Embroidering the Quilt

Refer to Embroidery Basics (page 110) for detailed information. Use *2 strands* of floss for all embroidery.

1. Refer to the project photo and use the vine placement pattern (page 22) to mark the wavy vine on the border of the quilt top with a water-soluble fabric marking pen. Freehand the tendrils and the position of the flowers. Be sure that the marking does not extend into the binding seam allowance (¼″ from the raw edge).

2. Layer the quilt top with the *batting only* and baste.

3. Backstitch the vine and tendrils through both layers using *green* floss.

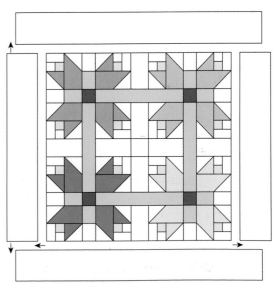

N. Border assembly

tickled pink mini quilt

Embroidery Patterns

Flower

Poinsettia (*optional*)

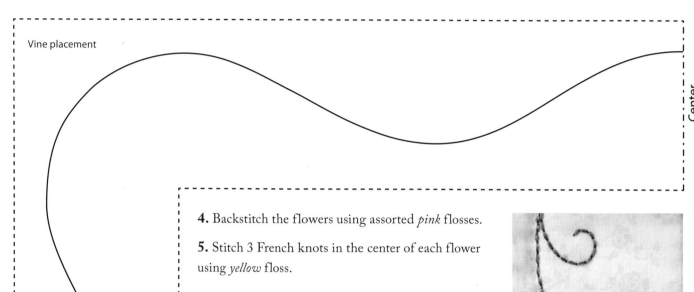

Vine placement

Center

Center

4. Backstitch the flowers using assorted *pink* flosses.

5. Stitch 3 French knots in the center of each flower using *yellow* floss.

Finishing the Quilt

1. Layer the embroidered and appliquéd quilt top with the backing fabric. Baste.

2. Quilt as desired. The featured quilt shows *cream* thread used to hand quilt down the center of the narrow sashing around the quilt center and alongside the embroidered vine.

3. Bind the quilt using the pink-and-green plaid binding strips. (Find additional information about binding a quilt at ctpub.com/quilting-sewing-tips.)

> ### tip
> For a Christmas version of this quilt, substitute red prints for the pink prints and stitch flowers with pointed petals to resemble poinsettias.

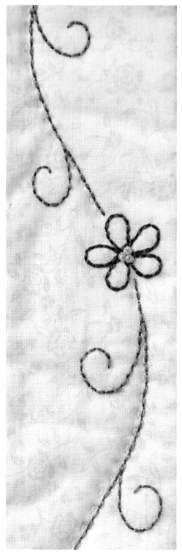

birdsong table runner

With simple wool appliqué surrounding scrappy on-point patchwork, this table runner celebrates the best of spring—blue skies, green leaves, and birdsong.

Materials

Cotton yardage is based on 40˝-wide fabric. Wool sizes are for felted wool. This pattern is scrap or precut friendly, though an entire precut pack or roll is not required. Precut sizes shown in the materials list indicate scrap sizes as well.

FABRICS

Cream prints: 12 assorted precut 10˝ squares *or* 46 assorted charm squares 5˝ × 5˝ for background

Pink, blue, and green prints: 9 assorted precut 10˝ squares of *each* color for center

Medium blue solid: 1½ yards for borders and binding

Backing: 1¾ yards

WOOL

Light brown: 1 fat eighth 9˝ × 22˝ for vines

Assorted greens: 4 squares 6˝ × 6˝ for leaves

Assorted ivory and ivory prints: 5 squares 5˝ × 5˝ for birds

Raspberry: 3˝ × 3˝ square for berries

Scraps of pink and blue: 10 squares 1½˝ × 1½˝ for wings

EMBROIDERY FLOSS

Colors to match wool

OTHER SUPPLIES

Batting: 30˝ × 62˝

Freezer paper

Cutting

CREAM PRINTS

From the precut 10″ squares or charm squares, cut:

- 8 squares 4⅞″ × 4⅞″, each cut in half diagonally twice to yield 32 setting triangles

- 36 squares 3″ × 3″ for the background

- 2 squares 2¾″ × 2¾″, each cut in half diagonally once to yield 4 corner triangles

PINK, BLUE, AND GREEN PRINTS

From each precut 10″ square, cut:

- 2 squares 3″ × 3″ for the table runner center

MEDIUM BLUE SOLID

On the lengthwise *grain of fabric (LOF), cut:*

- 3 strips 2¼″ × LOF for the binding

- 3 strips 4″ × LOF. Crosscut into:

  2 strips 4″ × 48″ for the border

  2 strips 4″ × 23″ for the border

LIGHT BROWN WOOL

- Cut 12 strips ¼″ × 22″ for the vines.

Assembling the Table Runner

Use a ¼″ seam allowance. Follow the pressing arrows provided in the diagram(s). For more information about pressing seam allowances, see Pressing Matters (page 19).

TABLE RUNNER CENTER

1. Lay out 52 assorted pink, blue, and green 3″ squares on point in a 4 × 13 setting and 36 assorted 3″ cream squares on point for the background. Add 30 assorted cream setting triangles to the ends of 16 diagonal rows, as shown. *Note:* Rows 4 and 13 have only 1 setting triangle.

2. Join the pieces in each diagonal row. Press all the seam allowances in each row to one side, alternating the direction in each row.

3. Join the rows.

4. Sew a cream corner triangle to each corner.

BORDERS

1. Measure the length of the table runner through the center from raw edge to raw edge. Trim the 48″ border strips to this length, and sew them to the long sides of the quilt.

2. Measure the width of the table runner across the center, including the borders just added. Trim the remaining 23″ border strips to this length, and sew them to the short sides of the quilt.

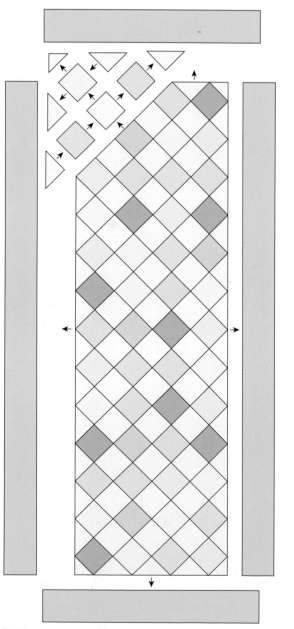

Table runner assembly

Appliquéing the Table Runner

Refer to Freezer-Paper Method (page 108) for step-by-step instructions. Refer to Stitching Wool Appliqués (page 109) as needed.

1. Use the Birdsong Table Runner appliqué patterns (below right) to prepare the wool appliqués.

2. Use the project photo as a guide to arrange *light-brown* wool strips on the borders of the table runner in a manner resembling a vine. Feel free to overlap and crisscross the sections of the vine or to cut smaller sections from the strips to create branches. As you arrange the vine, note that wherever 2 strips meet, the junction should later be covered by a leaf or a bird. In the same manner, plan to use a leaf to cover the exposed ends of the vines or branches. Be sure to keep the vine ⅜″ or more away from the raw edges of the borders to allow for the binding. When you are satisfied with the arrangement, pin the vine pieces to the borders and whipstitch them in place using *1 strand* of *light-brown* embroidery floss.

3. Position the remaining wool appliqués on the table runner borders as desired, covering vine junctions and ends and avoiding the seam allowance. Pin. Whipstitch the wool appliqués in place using *1 strand* of embroidery floss that matches the wool.

---

tip

If a project requires that you cut several of the same appliqué shape, such as leaves, first make a template by tracing the shape onto template plastic and cutting it out exactly on the drawn lines. It's much faster to use a template to draw shapes on freezer paper or fusible web than tracing each individual shape.

Finishing the Table Runner

1. Layer the appliquéd table runner top, batting, and backing. Baste.

2. Quilt as desired. The featured quilt shows *cream* thread used to hand quilt a crosshatch pattern in the table runner's center and to outline the wool appliqués on the outer border.

3. Bind the table runner using the medium-blue binding strips. (Find additional information about binding a quilt at ctpub.com/quilting-sewing-tips.)

---

birdsong table runner

Appliqué Patterns

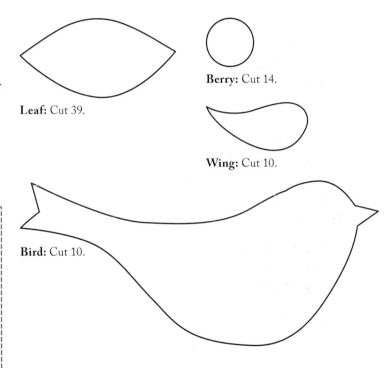

Leaf: Cut 39.

Berry: Cut 14.

Wing: Cut 10.

Bird: Cut 10.

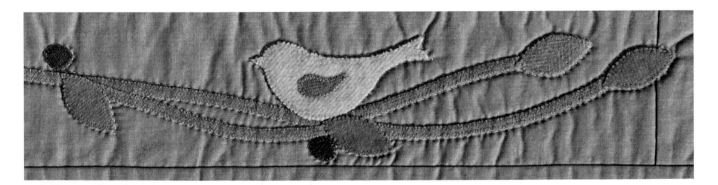

bloom quilt

This fresh and lovely lap quilt features pink Sister's Choice blocks and yellow buds that bloom against a warm white background. Showcase the stem and leaf border at either end of this quilt by draping Bloom *over a railing or the arm of a chair.*

Machine quilted by Joyce Lundrigan

Materials

Cotton yardage is based on 40˝-wide fabric. This pattern is scrap or precut friendly, though an entire precut pack is not required. Precut sizes shown in the materials list indicate scrap sizes as well.

FABRICS

Ivory print: 2⅔ yards for background

Pink prints: 11 assorted precut 10˝ squares* and 1 fat eighth 9˝ × 22˝ or 12 fat eighths for flower petals and Bud centers

Yellow prints: 8 assorted precut 10˝ squares for Bud blocks and flower centers

Green prints: 10 assorted fat eighths 9˝ × 22˝ for all blocks

Dark green print: ⅝ yard for flower borders and binding

Backing: 3½ yards

OTHER SUPPLIES

Batting: 61˝ × 70˝

*Cut the precut 10˝ squares carefully.

Cutting

IVORY PRINT

- Cut 4 strips 5″ × width of fabric (WOF). Crosscut into:

  25 squares 5″ × 5″ for the flower blocks

- Cut 9 strips 4¼″ × WOF. Crosscut into:

  8 strips 4¼″ × 11″ for the flower border sashing

  32 strips 4¼″ × 8″ for the sashing

- Cut 1 strip 3½″ × WOF. Crosscut into:

  20 rectangles 2″ × 3½″ for the stem and leaf blocks

- Cut 11 strips 2″ × WOF. Crosscut into:

  220 squares 2″ × 2″ (20 squares per strip) for the flower and stem and leaf blocks

- Cut 2 strips 1¾″ × WOF. Crosscut into:

  32 squares 1¾″ × 1¾″ for the Bud blocks

PINK PRINTS

From each of 11 fat eighths, cut:

- 2 squares 5″ × 5″ for the flower petals
- 8 squares 2″ × 2″ for the flower petals
- 2 squares 1¾″ × 1¾″ for the Bud centers (only 16 total needed)

From 1 fat eighth, cut:

- 3 squares 5″ × 5″ for the flower petals
- 12 squares 2″ × 2″ for the flower petals

  Sort the pink print squares into 25 flower petal sets. Each set will have:

  1 square 5″ × 5″

  4 squares 2″ × 2″

YELLOW PRINTS

From each of 8 precut 10″ squares, cut:

- 8 rectangles 1¾″ × 3″ for the Bud blocks

  Sort 4 matching yellow rectangles into a Bud petal set for a total of 16 sets.

- 4 squares 2″ × 2″ for the flower centers (only 25 total needed)

GREEN PRINTS

From each of 10 fat eighths, cut:

- 1 rectangle 2″ × 5″ for the stem
- 2 squares 3½″ × 3½″ for the leaves

  Keep the matching green print rectangle and squares (above) together as a stem and leaf block set.

- 12 squares 2″ × 2″ for the flower leaves
- 4 squares 1¾″ × 1¾″ for the Bud leaves (only 32 total needed)

DARK GREEN PRINT

- Cut 7 strips 2¼″ × WOF for the binding.
- Cut 2 strips 2″ × WOF. Crosscut into:

  8 rectangles 2″ × 4¼″ for the flower border

  20 squares 2″ × 2″ for the stem and leaf blocks

Making the Sister's Choice (Flower) Blocks

Use a ¼″ seam allowance. Follow the pressing arrows provided in the diagram(s). For more information about pressing seam allowances, see Pressing Matters (page 19).

FLOWER PETALS

1. Select 1 pink flower petal set and a 5″ ivory square. On the wrong side of the ivory square, use a pencil to lightly draw 2 diagonal lines from corner to corner, and 1 horizontal line and 1 vertical line through the center.

2. Layer the marked ivory square atop a 5″ pink square from the flower petal set, right sides together. Sew a scant ¼″ from each side of the diagonal lines. *fig. A*

3. Cut the pair apart on all drawn lines to make 8 half-square triangles. *fig. B*

4. Press the half-square triangles open. Trim to measure 2″ × 2″. *fig. C*

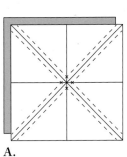

A.

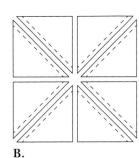

B.

C. Half-square triangle

5. Arrange 2 half-square triangles, 1 pink 2″ square (from the same flower petal set) and 1 ivory 2″ square into a four-patch configuration, as shown.

6. Join the pieces in each row; then join the rows together to make a flower petal unit. Make 4 flower petal units per set, for a total of 25 flower petal sets. *fig. D*

FLOWER LEAVES

1. Select 1 flower leaf set of 4 matching 2″ green squares. Sew 1 ivory 2″ square to 1 green 2″ square to make a flower leaf unit.

2. Make 4 flower leaf units. Keep these together as a set.

3. Repeat Steps 1 and 2 to make a total of 25 flower leaf sets. *fig. E*

ASSEMBLY

1. Arrange a set of flower petals, a set of flower leaves, and 1 yellow 2″ square, as shown. Be sure all the leaf units have green pointing away from the center and all the flower petal units are pointing outward.

2. Sew the top 2 flower petal units to the center leaf unit to make the top row. Repeat for the bottom row.

3. Sew 2 leaf units to opposite sides of the yellow center square to make a center row.

4. Join the top and bottom rows to the center row to make 1 Sister's Choice (flower) block measuring 8″ × 8″. *fig. F*

5. Make a total of 25 blocks.

Making the Bud Blocks

1. Use a pencil to lightly draw a diagonal line from corner to corner on the wrong side of 2 ivory 1¾″ squares and 2 matching 1¾″ green squares.

2. Select a Bud petal set of 4 matching yellow rectangles. Lay a marked square onto the end of each yellow rectangle, right sides together as shown. Stitch the pairs together on the drawn line. *fig. G*

3. Trim the seam allowances to ¼″. Make 2 yellow-and-ivory and 2 yellow-and-green rectangles. *figs. H & I*

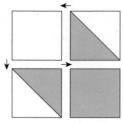

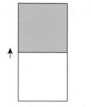

D. Flower petal unit

E. Flower leaf unit

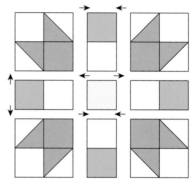

F. Sister's Choice (flower) block

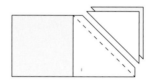

G.

H. Make 2.

I. Make 2.

4. With right sides together, layer a 1¾″ pink square atop 1 yellow-and-green rectangle as shown. Stitch the pair together with a partial seam, beginning at the middle of the pink square (reversing to lock stitches). Finger-press the seam allowances away from the pink square. *fig. J*

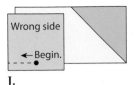

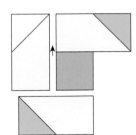

J.

5. Working in a counterclockwise direction and alternating ivory and green, join the other 3 rectangles to the sides of the pink center, sewing full seams across. Always finger-press the seam allowances away from pink square. *fig. K*

Note: When joining the last yellow-and-ivory rectangle to the center, make sure to fold the first rectangle out of the way before sewing.

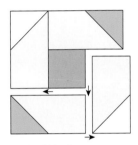

K.

6. Finish sewing the partial seam to complete the Bud block.

7. Make 16 Bud blocks, each measuring 4¼″ × 4¼″. *fig. L*

Making the Flower Borders

STEM AND LEAF BLOCKS

1. Use a pencil to lightly draw a diagonal line on the wrong side of 2 ivory and 2 dark green 2″ squares.

2. Select a green stem and leaf set. Layer a marked dark green square atop a corner of each matching 3½″ green square from the stem and leaf set, as shown. Stitch on the drawn lines.

3. In the same manner, stitch a marked ivory square to the opposite corner of each of the larger green squares. *fig. M*

4. Trim the seam allowances to ¼″ to make a pair of matching leaves. *fig. N*

5. Stitch an ivory rectangle to the top of each leaf of the matching pair. Be mindful of the orientation of the leaves.

6. Sew the green rectangle between the pair of leaves, as shown.

7. Make 10 stem and leaf blocks, each measuring 5″ × 8″. *fig. O*

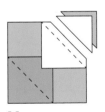

L. Bud block

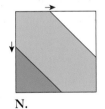

M. N.

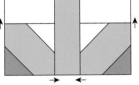

O. Stem and leaf block

ASSEMBLY

1. Match 10 stem and leaf blocks to 10 Sister's Choice (flower) blocks that contain the same green prints.

2. Making sure the green prints match in both blocks, stitch 1 stem and leaf block to a Sister's Choice block to make a flower border block. Repeat to make 10 flower border blocks. *fig. P*

3. To create the border sashing, sew a dark green rectangle to the short end of an 11″ ivory border sashing strip. Make 8 border sashing units. *fig. Q*

4. Join a row of 5 flower border blocks with 4 of the border sashing units, alternating positions as shown to make a flower border. Make 2. *fig. R*

Assembling the Quilt

1. Lay out 5 Sister's Choice blocks and 4 ivory 8″ sashing strips in alternating positions. Join the blocks and sashing to make a flower row. Make 3.

2. Lay out 5 ivory 8″ sashing strips and 4 Bud blocks in alternating positions. Join the sashing and blocks to make a Bud block row. Note that the direction of the Bud block alternates within each row. Make 4.

3. Lay out 4 Bud block rows and 3 flower rows, alternating positions and rotating the second and fourth Bud block rows 180°. Join the rows.

4. Sew a flower border to either end of the quilt center, as shown. *fig. S*

Finishing the Quilt

1. Layer the quilt top, batting, and backing. Baste.

2. Quilt as desired. The featured quilt was machine quilted using the edge-to-edge pattern Loralie by Anne Bright Designs.

3. Bind the quilt. (Find additional information about binding a quilt at ctpub.com/quilting-sewing-tips.)

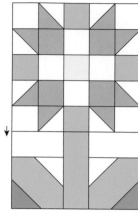
P. Flower border block

Q. Border sashing unit

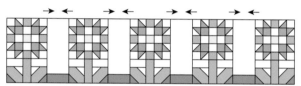
R. Flower border

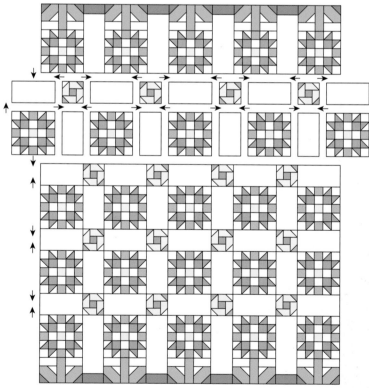
S. Quilt assembly

summer

Summertime in New England is short but sweet! The long days are filled with sunshine and blue skies, and at night, fireflies dance to the accompaniment of chirping crickets. Summer is for beach days and barbecues, berry picking and gardening, picnics and campfires— and it's made all the better because we know it won't last long!

little house—summer wallhanging

Back at Little House for the perfect summer day—blue skies, bright sunshine, colorful flowers, and a tire swing just waiting for the next rider!

Materials

Cotton yardage is based on 40˝-wide fabric. Wool sizes are for felted wool. This pattern is scrap or precut friendly, though an entire precut pack or roll is not required. Precut sizes shown in the materials list indicate scrap sizes as well.

FABRICS

Mottled blue: 1 precut 10˝ square for appliqué background

Green prints: ⅛ yard for single-fold binding

 4 assorted precut 2½˝ strips at least 9˝ long for quilt-center borders

 10 assorted mini charm squares 2½˝ × 2½˝ for Flying Geese backgrounds and bottom row sashing

 1 charm square 5˝ × 5˝ for Square-in-a-Square background

 3 assorted precut 10˝ squares for flower backgrounds

Medium and dark blue prints: 5 assorted mini charm squares 2½˝ × 2½˝ for top row blocks

 3 assorted charm squares 5˝ × 5˝ for flower blocks

Pale blue prints: 4 assorted mini charm squares 2½˝ × 2½˝ for Flying Geese

Yellow textured solid: 1 precut 2½˝ strip at least 14˝ long for flower centers

Backing: 1 fat quarter *or* 1 rectangle 12˝ × 16˝

FELTED WOOL

Green: 2˝ × 7˝ for grass

Dark red: 3˝ × 5˝ for house

Textured dark brown: 2˝ × 4˝ for roof

Medium brown: 2˝ × 4˝ for tree

Dark brown: 3˝ × 3˝ for windows and tire swing

Dark gold: 2˝ × 2˝ for door and chimney

Yellow: 1½˝ × 1½˝ for sun

Light brown: Scrap for window boxes

Medium blue: Scrap for flowerpots

EMBROIDERY FLOSS

Colors to match wool

Light blue: 2 shades for flowers

Red and white for flag

OTHER SUPPLIES

Batting: 12˝ × 16˝

Lightweight paper-backed fusible web (17˝ wide): ¼ yard

Foundation paper for paper piecing

Small bird button (I used the Tiny Bluebird from Just Another Button Company.)

Water-soluble fabric marking pen

Cutting

MOTTLED BLUE

- Cut 1 square 8″ × 8″ for the appliqué center.

GREEN PRINTS

From yardage, cut:

- 2 strips 1¼″ × width of fabric (WOF) for the binding

From 4 assorted precut 2½″ strips, cut the quilt-center borders:

- 2 strips 1¼″ × 8″
- 2 strips 1¼″ × 6½″

From 10 assorted mini charm squares, cut:

- 8 squares 2¼″ × 2¼″, each cut in half diagonally once to make 8 triangle *pairs* (B)
- 2 assorted rectangles 1¼″ × 2½″ for the bottom row sashing

From 1 charm square, cut:

- 1 *set* of 2 squares 2¼″ × 2¼″, each cut in half diagonally once to make 4 matching print triangles (D)

From each of 3 assorted precut 10″ squares, cut:

- 1 *set* of 6 squares 2¼″ × 2¼″, each cut in half diagonally once to make 12 matching background triangles (F)

MEDIUM AND DARK BLUE PRINTS

From 5 assorted mini charm squares, cut:

- 4 rectangles 1½″ × 2½″ (A)
- 1 square 1¾″ × 1¾″ (C)

From each of 3 assorted charm squares, cut 1 set of:

- 4 squares 1¾″ × 1¾″ (E)

PALE BLUE PRINTS

- Cut 4 rectangles 1½″ × 2½″ (A).

YELLOW TEXTURED SOLID

- Cut 6 squares 2″ × 2″, each cut in half diagonally once to make 12 triangles (G).

> ## tip
>
> To display these charming wallhangings, find a quilt hanger so you can rotate your Little Houses as the seasons change. But if you can't bear to put them away, the Little House series is striking hanging all in a row!

The Quilt Center

Because of the small pieces and the narrow, sharp points of the tree branches, the fusible web method for wool appliqué is most suitable. Refer to Fusible Web Method (page 109) for step-by-step instructions. Refer to Stitching Wool Appliqués (page 109) as needed.

APPLIQUÉ

1. Use the general Little House Wallhanging appliqué patterns (page 13) for the house, roof, windows, door, chimney, tree, and grass, and the Little House—Summer Wallhanging appliqué patterns (page 37) for the sun, tire swing, window box, and flowerpot to prepare the wool appliqués.

2. In the center of the mottled blue fabric, draw a 6½″ × 6½″ square with a water-soluble marking pen. This square is the appliqué placement area, *including* the ¼″ seam allowance, and will be the trim size after the appliqué and embroidery have been completed. (The finished size will measure 6″ x 6″.)

3. Use the project photo as a guide to position the wool appliqués within the drawn square. Make sure that the house is centered from left to right and that the grass will be enclosed within the seams of the finished project.

Note: Certain appliqué pieces overlap, so be sure to tuck the bottom layer of pieces under the top layers before fusing. For example, the grass overlaps the bottom edges of the house and door.

4. Once you are satisfied with the placement of the wool appliqués, fuse the pieces to the background.

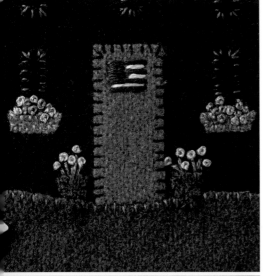

5. Whipstitch the wool appliqués in place using *1 strand* of embroidery floss. Use *gold* floss for the house and windows and *dark brown* floss for the door. For the remaining appliqués, match the floss color to the wool color. It isn't necessary to whipstitch the bottom and side edges of the grass because they'll be enclosed within the seams of the finished project.

6. For the tire swing, wrap the wool circle with stitches by bringing the needle up on the outside of the tire, laying the floss over the top of the tire, and then reinserting the needle down through the inside of the tire, continuing in the same manner around the circumference of the tire.

EMBROIDERY

Refer to Embroidery Basics (page 110) for detailed information. Use 2 *strands* of floss for all embroidery unless otherwise indicated.

1. Trace the dashed lines of the tree branches and the sun's rays (see the Little House Wallhanging appliqué patterns, page 13, and the Little House—Summer Wallhanging appliqué patterns, page 37) onto the fabric using the water-soluble fabric marking pen.

2. Backstitch the tree branches using *medium brown* floss.

3. Embroider the leaves along the tree branches using *green* floss and lazy daisy stitches. Use the same green floss to backstitch sunflower stems with lazy daisy leaves along the side of the house and to stitch a single straight stitch (one each) for flower stems along the top edge of the flowerpots that flank the front door.

4. Stitch French knots for the sunflower centers using *dark brown* floss.

5. Make the sunflower petals using *yellow* floss and straight stitches radiating out and around the brown French knots. Also use the yellow floss to stitch French knots for the flowerpot flowers and to backstitch rays around the sun.

6. Stitch French knots for the window box flowers using *light blue* floss.

7. Use *red, white, and medium blue* floss and long straight stitches to stitch the American flag on the front door.

8. Backstitch a rope for the tire swing using *light brown* floss.

TRIMMING

Trim the appliquéd and embroidered quilt center to 6½″ × 6½″ along the marked lines you drew on the fabric previously.

Making the Paper-Pieced Blocks

Photocopy or download and print the project patterns (see Foundation Paper-Piecing Patterns, page 10).

Copy the Little House Wallhanging top row foundation patterns (page 12) and Little House—Summer Wallhanging bottom row foundation patterns (page 37) onto foundation paper. Cut out each pattern ¼″ beyond its outer dashed line. Refer to Paper-Piecing Basics (page 105) for step-by-step instructions.

TOP ROW BLOCKS

1. Paper piece 2 Flying Geese units *(fig. A)*, covering the areas in numerical order. Use the pieces designated for each area as follows:

> **Areas 1 and 7:** Medium or dark blue rectangles (A)
>
> **Areas 4 and 10:** Pale blue rectangles (A)
>
> **Areas 2 and 3, 5 and 6, 8 and 9, 11 and 12:** Green triangle pairs (B)

2. Paper piece 1 Square-in-a-Square block *(fig. B)*, covering the areas in numerical order. Use the pieces designated for each area as follows:

> **Area 1:** Blue square (C)
>
> **Areas 2, 3, 4, and 5:** 1 set of 4 matching green triangles (D)

BOTTOM ROW BLOCKS

1. Note that each flower is comprised of 4 petals. Paper piece 4 flower petals, covering the areas in numerical order using the pieces designated as follows:

> **Area 1:** 1 set of 4 medium or dark blue squares (E)
>
> **Areas 2, 3, and 4:** 1 set of green triangles (F)
>
> **Area 5:** 4 yellow triangles (G)

2. Join 4 flower petals together with the yellow triangles meeting in the center to make 1 flower block. Gently remove the paper from behind the block and press the seam allowances open. Repeat to make 3 flower blocks. *fig. C*

A. Flying Geese unit

B. Square-in-a-Square

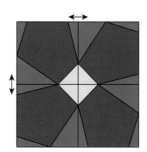

C. Flower block

summertime pillow

With its brightly colored patchwork surrounding a pretty wool flower, this cheery pillow is a celebration of summer.

Materials

Cotton yardage is based on 40˝-wide fabric. Wool sizes are for felted wool.

FABRICS

Assorted summer prints: 1 mini charm square pack *or* 42 squares 2½˝ × 2½˝ (I used Floral Gatherings by Primitive Gatherings.)

Green print: ½ yard for pillow backing

Lining fabric: ½ yard of muslin

Cream solid: 5˝ × 7˝ for pillow inset

FELTED WOOL

Pink: 4˝ × 4˝ for flower

Green: 3˝ × 3˝ for stem and leaves

Yellow: 1˝ × 1˝ for flower center

EMBROIDERY FLOSS

Colors to match wool

OTHER SUPPLIES

Batting: 16˝ × 20˝

Pillow form: 12˝ × 16˝

Freezer paper

Water-soluble fabric marking pen

Cutting

ASSORTED SUMMER PRINTS

- Cut 42 squares 2½″ × 2½″ if you've chosen not to use a mini charm square pack.

GREEN PRINT

- Cut 2 backing panels 12″ × 12½″.

LINING FABRIC

- Cut 1 rectangle 16″ × 20″.

CREAM SOLID

- Cut 1 rectangle 5″ × 7″.

Making the Pillow Top

Use a ¼″ seam allowance. Follow the pressing arrows provided in the diagram(s). For more information about pressing seam allowances, see Pressing Matters (page 19).

PILLOW INSET APPLIQUÉ

Refer to Freezer-Paper Method (page 108) for step-by-step instructions and to Stitching Wool Appliqués (page 109) as needed.

1. Cut 1 strip of green wool ³⁄₁₆″ × 3″ for the stem.

2. Use the Summertime Pillow appliqué patterns (page 40) to prepare the wool appliqués.

3. With a water-soluble marking pen, draw a 4½″ × 6½″ rectangle centered on the cream rectangle. The rectangle is the appliqué placement area, *including* the ¼″ seam allowance, and will be the trim size after the appliqué has been completed. (The finished size will measure 4″ × 6″.)

4. Use the project photo close-up as a guide to position the wool appliqués within the drawn rectangle. Pin. Before stitching, make sure that the bottom edge of the flower stem rests on the drawn line of the rectangle. This way it will be enclosed within the seam of the finished project.

5. Whipstitch the wool appliqués in place using *1 strand* of embroidery floss that matches the wool.

6. Trim the pillow inset to 4½″ × 6½″ using the lines you marked in Step 3.

PILLOW TOP ASSEMBLY

1. Lay out the appliquéd pillow inset and the 42 squares as shown.

2. When you are happy with the arrangement, join the squares into rows; then join the rows.

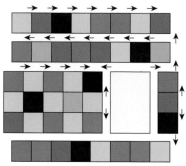

Pillow top assembly

EMBROIDERY

Refer to Embroidery Basics (page 110) for detailed information.

1. Use the Summertime Pillow embroidery pattern (below right) to mark the lettering on the pillow inset with the water-soluble fabric marking pen. A lightbox or other light source is helpful.

2. Layer the pillow top, batting, and lining fabric. Baste.

3. Backstitch the lettering on the pillow inset through all layers using *2 strands* of *green* floss.

QUILTING

1. Quilt the pillow top as desired. The featured pillow was machine quilted ¼″ along both sides of each seam, stopping or starting at the inset as necessary and knotting the thread ends at the back (lining side) of the pillow top.

2. Trim the batting and lining even with the pillow top.

Finishing the Pillow

1. To make the pillow back, hem one of the 12½″ edges of each backing panel. To do this, fold the edge toward the wrong side ⅜″ and then ⅜″ again, and press.

2. Stitch close to the inside folded edge.

3. Layer one backing panel on the pillow top, right sides together and raw edges aligned.

4. Layer the remaining panel on the opposite side of the pillow top, right sides together and raw edges aligned. Pin.

5. Stitch around all the edges and through all the layers with a ¼″ seam.

6. Trim the corners to reduce bulk, turn the pillow right side out, and insert the pillow form.

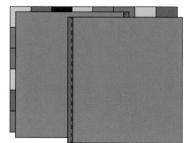

Pillow assembly

---

summertime pillow

Appliqué Patterns

Cut 1 of each except where noted.

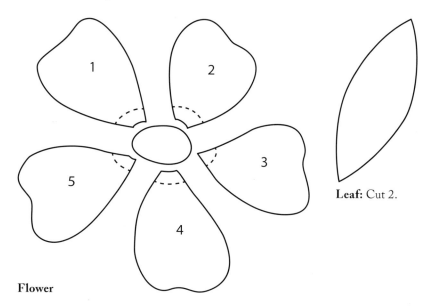

Flower

Leaf: Cut 2.

Embroidery Pattern

SUMMER

Pillow lettering

strawberry blossoms mini quilt

When my three kids were little, they loved to picnic. This quilt reminds me of those lazy summer days and the wild strawberries that grew along the edges of our yard.

Materials

Cotton yardage is based on 40″-wide fabric.

FABRIC

Red print: ⅜ yard for borders and binding

Light red solid: 1 fat eighth 9″ × 22″

Dark red solid: 1 fat eighth 9″ × 22″

Ivory solid: 1 fat eighth 9″ × 22″

Ivory prints: 8 assorted rectangles 3″ × 5″ for blossoms

Green prints: 6 assorted squares 3″ × 3″ for leaves

Backing: 1 fat quarter *or* 1 rectangle 18″ × 22″

EMBROIDERY FLOSS

Yellow for flower centers

Green perle cotton #8 for vine

Ecru perle cotton #12 for big-stitch quilting

OTHER SUPPLIES

Batting: 18″ × 18″

Lightweight paper-backed fusible web (17″ wide): ⅓ yard

Template plastic

Water-soluble fabric marking pen

forget-me-not table runner

Scrappy paper-pieced flowers seem to spin and dance in a field of green encircled by a pretty wool vine. This table runner was inspired by the tiny blue wildflowers that bloomed on the banks of a stream near my childhood home.

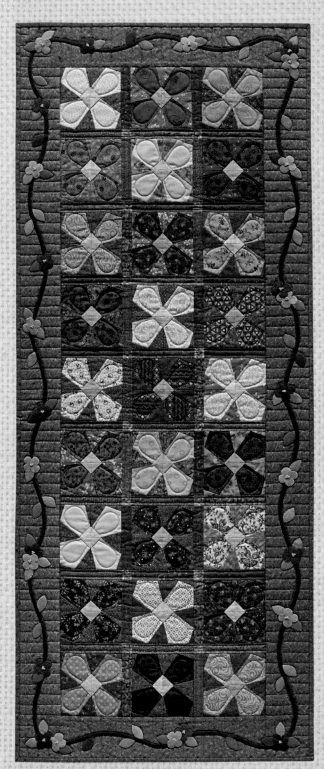

Machine quilted by Joyce Lundrigan

Materials

Cotton yardage is based on 40˝-wide fabric. Wool sizes are for felted wool. This pattern is scrap or precut friendly, though an entire precut pack or roll is not required. Precut sizes shown in the materials list indicate scrap sizes as well.

FABRIC

Green prints: 1½ yards for borders and binding

27 assorted precut 10˝ squares for backgrounds

12 assorted charm squares 5˝ × 5˝ for sashing

8 assorted mini charm squares 2½˝ × 2½˝ for cornerstones

Light blue prints: 14 assorted precut 10˝ squares for flowers

Medium blue prints: 13 assorted precut 10˝ squares for flowers

Yellow prints: 7 assorted precut 10˝ squares for flower centers

Backing: 1¾ yards

WOOL

Dark green: 5˝ × 11˝ for vine

Greens: 6 assorted squares 6˝ × 6˝ for leaves

Light and medium blue: 3 assorted squares 6˝ × 6˝ for border flowers

EMBROIDERY FLOSS

Colors to match wool

Yellow

OTHER SUPPLIES

Batting: 30˝ × 61˝

Foundation paper for paper piecing

Freezer paper

Cutting

GREEN PRINTS

Cut on the lengthwise *grain of fabric (LOF) for the following:*

From yardage, cut:

- 3 strips 3½″ × LOF. Crosscut into:

  2 strips 3½″ × 47″ for the border

  2 strips 3½″ × 21½″ for the border

- 3 strips 2¼″ × LOF for the binding

From each precut 10″ square, cut 1 set of flower backgrounds:

  4 rectangles 2″ × 3″ (B)

  8 rectangles 1½″ × 2½″ (C)

From 12 assorted charm squares, cut:

- 42 sashing strips 1¼″ × 5″

From 8 assorted mini charm squares, cut:

- 16 cornerstones 1¼″ × 1¼″

LIGHT BLUE PRINTS

From each precut 10″ square, cut 1 set of flower petals:

- 4 squares 3″ × 3″ (A)

MEDIUM BLUE PRINTS

From each precut 10″ square, cut 1 set of flower petals:

- 4 squares 3″ × 3″ (A)

YELLOW PRINTS

From each precut 10″ square, cut 4 sets of:

- 2 squares 2¼″ × 2¼″, each cut in half diagonally once to make 4 triangles (D)

  4 matching triangles make 1 set.

DARK GREEN WOOL

- Cut 15 strips ¼″ × 11″ for the vine.

Making the Flower Blocks

Photocopy or download and print the project patterns (see Foundation Paper-Piecing Patterns, page 10).

Make 27 copies of the Forget-Me-Not Table Runner foundation patterns (page 47) onto foundation paper. Cut out each pattern ¼″ beyond its outer dashed line. Refer to Paper-Piecing Basics (page 105) for step-by-step instructions.

1. Note that each flower is comprised of 4 petals. Select 1 set of light- or medium-blue flower petals (A), 1 set of flower backgrounds (B, C), and 1 set of yellow triangles (D) to complete a flower block.

2. Paper piece 4 flower petals, covering the areas in numerical order. Use the pieces designated for each area as follows:

  Area 1: Blue square (A)

  Areas 2 and 3: Green rectangles (C)

  Area 4: Green rectangle (B)

  Area 5: Yellow triangle (D)

3. Join 4 matching flower petals to make a flower block. Gently remove the paper from behind the block and press the seam allowances open. Repeat to make 27 flower blocks.

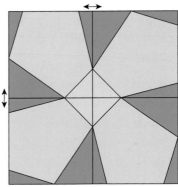

Flower block

garden party quilt

Whimsical flowers in vibrant shades of red, pink, and orange peek through a green lattice of Irish Chain blocks. With use, the raw edges of the flower appliqués on this cheerful quilt take on a charming, shabby-chic look.

Machine quilted by
Joyce Lundrigan

Materials

Cotton yardage is based on 40˝-wide fabric. This pattern is scrap or precut friendly, though an entire precut pack or roll is not required. Precut sizes shown in the materials list indicate scrap sizes as well.

FABRICS

Light tan print: 2¼ yards for backgrounds

Green prints: 16 assorted precut 10˝ squares for blocks

Red prints: 8 assorted precut 10˝ squares for appliqués

Pink prints: 8 assorted precut 10˝ squares for appliqués

Orange prints: 8 assorted precut 10˝ squares for appliqués

Yellow print: 1 fat quarter for flower centers

Green print: 1 yard for border and binding

Backing: 4 yards

OTHER SUPPLIES

Batting: 64˝ × 64˝

Lightweight paper-backed fusible web (17˝ wide): 2¼ yards

Dark pink and yellow thread for machine appliqué

Cutting

LIGHT TAN PRINT

- Cut 5 strips 8″ × width of fabric (WOF). Crosscut into:

  24 squares 8″ × 8″ for the appliqué background squares

- Cut 5 strips 2″ × WOF. Crosscut into:

  84 squarcs 2″ × 2″

- Cut 5 strips 5″ × WOF. Crosscut into:

  84 rectangles 2″ × 5″

GREEN PRINTS FOR BLOCKS

From each of 12 assorted precut 10″ squares, cut:

- 1 rectangle 2″ × 8″
- 1 rectangle 2″ × 5″
- 11 squares 2″ × 2″

From each of 4 assorted precut 10″ squares, cut:

- 1 rectangle 2″ × 3½″
- 1 rectangle 2″ × 6½″
- 10 squares 2″ × 2″

Sort the green pieces by size.

GREEN PRINT FOR BORDER AND BINDING

- Cut 8 strips 2″ × WOF for the borders. Crosscut into:

  4 strips 2″ × 26¾″

  4 strips 2″ × 28¼″

- Cut 6 strips 2¼″ × WOF for the binding.

Making the Flower Blocks

APPLIQUÉ PREPARATION

The following instructions are for raw-edge fusible appliqué. If you prefer to use a different method of appliqué, note that the patterns (page 52) do not include seam allowances.

1. Use the Garden Party Quilt appliqué patterns (page 52) to trace each appliqué shape onto the paper side of lightweight fusible web, leaving ½″ between shapes.

2. Cut out the shapes roughly ¼″ outside the drawn lines.

3. Place the shapes, fusible web side down, on the wrong side of the appropriate fabric to yield a *set* of 5 matching flower petals from *each* of the 8 red, 8 pink, and 8 orange prints and 24 yellow flower centers.

4. Following the manufacturer's instructions, fuse the shapes to the fabric.

5. Cut out each shape exactly on the drawn lines and remove the paper.

APPLIQUÉ

1. Use the appliqué placement diagram as a guide to arrange 5 matching flower petals, adhesive side down, on a light-tan appliqué background square. As you lay out the petals, be sure that the outside curves of the petals are at least ½″ from the raw edges of the background square.

---

tip

The junction of the five petals and the yellow centers of the flowers should be ¼″ below the center of the 8″ background square so that the petals are equidistant from the four edges of the block.

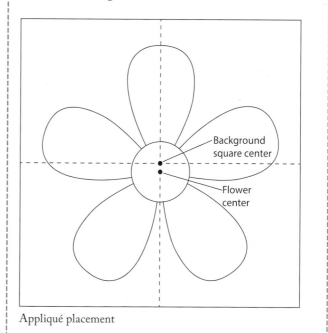

Appliqué placement

Note: *If you prefer to use a full-size appliqué placement diagram, a pdf for the* Garden Party Quilt *project is available for download (see Foundation Paper-Piecing Patterns, page 10).*

2. When you are satisfied with your arrangement, fuse only the *petals* in place.

3. Thread your sewing machine with dark pink thread. Straight stitch around each petal ⅛″ inside the raw edge. Make sure to start and stop sewing at the point of each petal at the flower's center. Backstitch to secure your threads. Trim the thread ends close to the fabric.

4. Place a yellow flower center in the center of the flower. Remember that the center of the flower does not align with the center of the background square. Fuse in place.

5. Thread your sewing machine with yellow thread. Straight stitch around the flower center ⅛″ inside the raw edge. When sewing the flower center, do not backstitch at the beginning and end of your stitching. Instead, leave the thread ends long and use a sewing needle to move the threads to the back of the fabric. Knot the thread ends at the back of the block and trim.

6. Repeat to make 8 red, 8 pink, and 8 orange flower blocks for a total of 24 flower blocks.

Flower appliqué

Making the Irish Chain Blocks

Use a ¼″ seam allowance. Follow the pressing arrows provided in the diagram(s). For more information about pressing seam allowances, see Pressing Matters (page 19).

Each block should display a variety of green prints.

CENTER BLOCKS

1. Arrange 5 green and 4 light tan 2″ squares into 3 rows of 3 squares each, as shown.

2. Join the squares in each row. Join the rows together to make a nine-patch unit.

3. Repeat Steps 1 and 2 to make 13 nine-patch units. *fig. A*

4. Sew a 5″ light tan rectangle to the left and right sides of a nine-patch unit.

5. Sew 2 green 2″ squares to opposite ends of a 5″ light tan rectangle to make a border strip. Make 2.

6. Sew a border strip to the top and bottom of the nine-patch unit to make a center block.

7. Repeat to make 13 center blocks, each measuring 8″ × 8″. *fig. B*

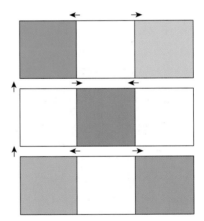

A. Nine-patch

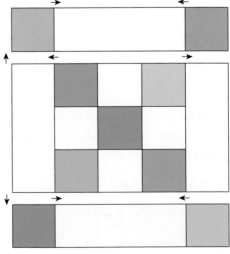

B. Center block

EDGE BLOCKS

1. Arrange 3 green and 3 light tan 2″ squares into 2 rows of 3 squares, as shown.

2. Join the squares in each row. Join the rows together.

3. Sew a 5″ green rectangle to the top to make an edge block center. *fig. C*

4. Sew a 5″ light tan rectangle to the left and right sides of the edge block center.

5. Sew 2 green 2″ squares to opposite ends of a 5″ light tan rectangle. Sew this strip to the bottom of the edge block center.

6. Sew an 8″ green rectangle to the top of the unit.

7. Repeat to make 8 edge blocks, each measuring 8″ × 8″. *fig. D*

CORNER BLOCKS

1. Arrange 2 green and 2 light tan 2″ squares into 2 rows of 2 squares, as shown.

2. Join the squares in each row. Join the rows together to make a four-patch unit. *fig. E*

3. Sew a 3½″ green rectangle to the top of a four-patch unit, as shown. Note the four-patch unit orientation!

4. Sew a 5″ green rectangle to the left of the four-patch unit.

5. Sew a 5″ light tan rectangle to the bottom of the four-patch unit.

6. Sew 1 green 2″ square to the end of a 5″ light tan rectangle. Sew this strip to the right side of the original four-patch unit.

7. Sew a 6½″ green rectangle to the top of the unit, centered above the first green rectangle sewn to the four-patch unit.

8. Sew an 8″ green rectangle to the left side of the unit to make a corner block.

9. Repeat to make 4 corner blocks, each measuring 8″ × 8″. *fig. F*

Assembling the Quilt

QUILT CENTER

1. Using the quilt assembly diagram as a guide, lay out the 24 flower blocks, 13 center blocks, 8 edge blocks, and 4 corner blocks in 7 rows of 7 blocks each, as shown.

2. Join the blocks in each row.

3. Join the rows. The quilt center should measure 53″ square.

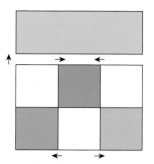

C. Edge block center

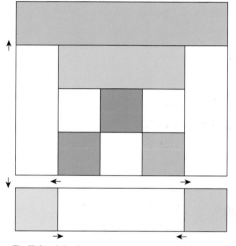

D. Edge block

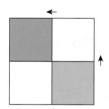

E. Four-patch

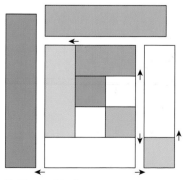

F. Corner block

BORDERS

1. Join together 2 border strips 26¾˝ end to end to make a 53˝ border strip. Press the seam allowances open. Repeat to make a second 53˝ border strip.

2. Matching the centers, sew a 53˝ border strip to the left and right sides of the quilt center.

3. Join together 2 border strips 28¼˝ end to end to make a 56˝ border strip. Press the seam allowances open. Repeat to make a second 56˝ border strip.

4. Matching the centers, sew a 56˝ border strip to the top and bottom of the quilt center.

Finishing the Quilt

1. Layer the quilt top, batting, and backing. Baste.

2. Quilt as desired. The featured quilt was machine quilted with diagonal lines through the centers of the Irish Chain blocks, a triple-leaf pattern on each side of the Irish Chain blocks, outline quilting around each flower, and a wavy-leaf pattern in the outer border.

3. Bind the quilt using the green binding strips. (Find additional information about binding a quilt at ctpub.com/quilting-sewing-tips.)

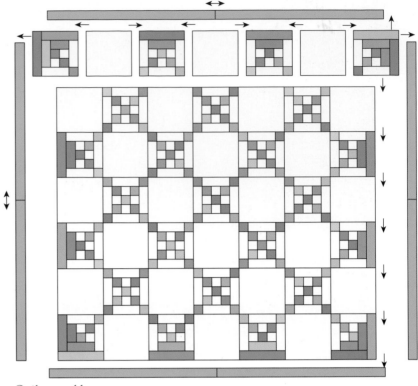

Quilt assembly

---

garden party quilt

Appliqué Patterns

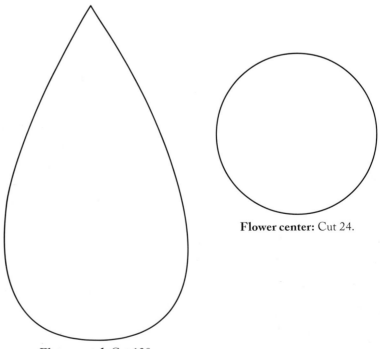

Flower center: Cut 24.

Flower petal: Cut 120.

fall

Before you know it, the days grow shorter, the air cools, and suddenly it's fall. And fall in New England is glorious! Picking apples and baking pies, hiking mountains just to admire the foliage, the smell of spice and wood smoke in the air, and the sound of geese flying overhead—fall is a feast for the senses.

little house—fall wallhanging

It's fall at Little House. The leaves are changing color, the pumpkins are waiting to be carved, and geese fly south through clear, blue skies.

Materials

Cotton yardage is based on 40˝-wide fabric. Wool sizes are for felted wool. This pattern is scrap or precut friendly, though an entire precut pack or roll is not required. Precut sizes shown in the materials list indicate scrap sizes as well.

FABRICS

Slate-blue print: 1 precut 10˝ square for appliqué background

Brown prints: ⅛ yard for single-fold binding

4 assorted precut 2½˝ strips at least 9˝ long for quilt-center borders

4 assorted charm squares 5˝ × 5˝ for Maple Leaf and Square-in-a-Square backgrounds

10 assorted mini charm squares 2½˝ × 2½˝ for Flying Geese backgrounds and bottom row sashing

Red prints: 2 assorted charm squares 5˝ × 5˝ for Maple Leaf blocks

5 assorted mini charm squares 2½˝ × 2½˝ for top row blocks

Orange prints: 1 charm square 5˝ × 5˝ for Maple Leaf block

4 assorted mini charm squares 2½˝ × 2½˝ for top row blocks

Light brown print: 1 mini charm square 2½˝ × 2½˝ for Maple Leaf stems

Backing: 1 fat quarter *or* 1 rectangle 12˝ × 16˝

FELTED WOOL

Dark green: 2˝ × 7˝ for grass

Dark red: 3˝ × 5˝ for house

Textured dark brown: 2˝ × 4˝ for roof

Medium brown: 2˝ × 4˝ for tree

Dark brown: 2˝ × 2˝ for windows

Dark gold: 2˝ × 2˝ for door and chimney

Tan: Scrap for hay bales

Light brown: Scrap for pineapple

Orange: Scrap for pumpkins

EMBROIDERY FLOSS

Colors to match wool

Red and rust for leaves

Gray for smoke and geese

OTHER SUPPLIES

Batting: 12˝ × 16˝

Lightweight paper-backed fusible web (17˝ wide): ¼ yard

Foundation paper for paper piecing

Small bird button (I used the Tiny Rook from Just Another Button Company.)

Water-soluble fabric marking pen

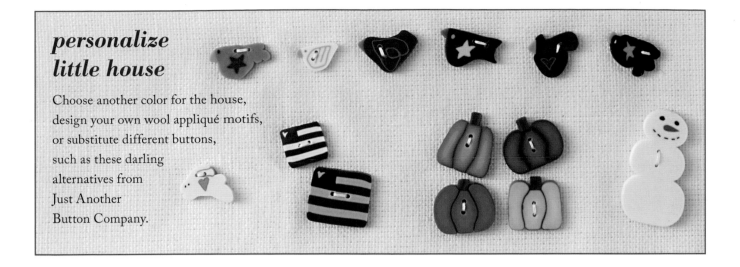

Cutting

SLATE-BLUE PRINT

- Cut 1 square 8″ × 8″ for the appliqué center.

BROWN PRINTS

From yardage, cut:

- 2 strips 1¼″ × width of fabric (WOF) for the binding

From 4 assorted precut 2½″ strips, cut the quilt-center borders:

- 2 strips 1¼″ × 8″
- 2 strips 1¼″ × 6½″

From 1 charm square, cut 1 set of:

- 2 squares 2¼″ × 2¼″, each cut in half diagonally once to make 4 matching print triangles (D)

From each of 3 assorted charm squares, cut 1 set of:

- 3 squares 2¼″ × 2¼″, each cut in half diagonally once to make 6 matching print triangles (H)
- 1 square 1½″ × 1½″ (G)

From 10 assorted mini charm squares, cut:

- 8 squares 2¼″ × 2¼″, each cut in half diagonally once to make 8 triangle *pairs* (B)
- 2 assorted rectangles 1¼″ × 2½″ for the bottom row sashing

RED PRINTS

From each of 2 assorted charm squares, carefully cut 1 set of:

- 2 squares 2¼″ × 2¼″, each cut in half diagonally once to make 4 matching print triangles (F)
- 3 squares 1½″ × 1½″ (E)

From 5 assorted mini charm squares, cut:

- 4 rectangles 1½″ × 2½″ (A)
- 1 square 1¾″ × 1¾″ (C)

ORANGE PRINTS

From 1 charm square, carefully cut 1 set of:

- 2 squares 2¼″ × 2¼″, each cut in half diagonally once to make 4 matching print triangles (F)
- 3 squares 1½″ × 1½″ (E)

From 4 assorted mini charm squares, cut:

- 4 rectangles 1½″ × 2½″ (A)

LIGHT BROWN PRINT

From 1 mini charm square, carefully cut:

- 3 rectangles ¾″ × 1½″ (I)

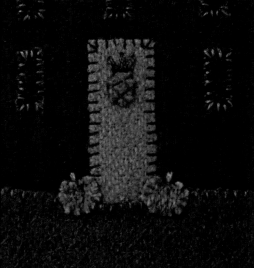

The Quilt Center

Follow the pressing arrows provided in the diagram(s). For more information about pressing seam allowances, see Pressing Matters (page 19).

Because of the small pieces and the narrow, sharp points of the tree branches, the fusible web method for wool appliqué is suggested for this project. Refer to Fusible Web Method (page 109) for step-by-step instructions. Refer to Stitching Wool Appliqués (page 109) as needed.

APPLIQUÉ

1. Use the general Little House Wallhanging appliqué patterns (page 13) for the house, roof, windows, door, chimney, tree, and grass, and the Little House—Fall Wallhanging appliqué patterns (page 59) for the pineapple, pumpkin, and hay bale to prepare the wool appliqués.

2. In the center of the slate-blue fabric, draw a 6½″ × 6½″ square with a water-soluble marking pen. This square is the appliqué placement area, *including* the ¼″ seam allowance, and will be the trim size after the appliqué and embroidery have been completed. (The finished size will measure 6″ × 6″.)

3. Use the project photo as a guide to position the wool appliqués within the drawn square. Make sure that the house is centered from left to right and that the grass will be enclosed within the seams of the finished project.

Note: Certain appliqué pieces overlap, so be sure to tuck the bottom layer of pieces under the top layers before fusing. For example, the grass overlaps the bottom edges of the house and door.

4. Once you are satisfied with the placement of the wool appliqués, fuse the pieces to the background.

5. Whipstitch the wool appliqués in place using *1 strand* of embroidery floss. Use *gold* floss for the house and windows and *dark brown* floss for the door. For the remaining appliqués, match the floss to the wool. It isn't necessary to whipstitch the bottom and side edges of the grass because they'll be enclosed within the seams of the finished project.

EMBROIDERY

Refer to Embroidery Basics (page 110) for detailed information. Use *2 strands* of floss for all embroidery unless otherwise indicated.

1. Trace the dashed lines of the tree branches (see the Little House Wallhanging appliqué patterns, page 13) onto the fabric using the water-soluble fabric marking pen.

2. Backstitch the rake handle and tree branches using *medium brown* floss. Use the same medium brown floss and a long straight stitch to stitch the rake tines; use the same floss and tiny straight stitches for the pumpkins stems.

3. Use a combination of *red-, orange-, and rust-colored* floss to stitch lazy daisies for the leaves along the tree branches and on the grass below the tree.

4. Backstitch the creases on the pumpkins using *1 strand* of *orange* floss.

5. Use *green* floss to stitch tiny straight stitches above the pineapple for the pineapple's leaves.

6. Create highlights with *1 strand* of *dark brown* floss by stitching long straight stitches diagonally across the pineapple and horizontally across the bales of hay.

7. Backstitch a curving line of smoke rising from the chimney using *gray* floss. Use *1 strand* of the same gray floss to stitch tiny straight stitches in the shape of *V*'s for the geese.

TRIMMING

Trim the appliquéd and embroidered quilt center to 6½″ × 6½″ along the marked lines you drew on the fabric previously.

Making the Paper-Pieced Blocks

Photocopy or download and print the project patterns (see Foundation Paper-Piecing Patterns, page 10).

Copy the Little House Wallhanging top row foundation patterns (page 12) and Little House—Fall Wallhanging bottom row foundation patterns (page 59) onto foundation paper. Cut out each pattern ¼″ beyond its outer dashed line. Refer to Paper-Piecing Basics (page 105) for step-by-step instructions.

TOP ROW BLOCKS

1. Paper piece 2 Flying Geese units *(fig. A)*, covering the areas in numerical order. Use the pieces designated for each area as follows:

Areas 1 and 7: Red rectangles (A)

Areas 2 and 3, 5 and 6, 8 and 9, 11 and 12: Brown triangle pairs (B)

Areas 4 and 10: Orange rectangles (A)

2. Paper piece 1 Square-in-a-Square block *(fig. B)*, covering the areas in numerical order. Use the pieces designated for each area as follows:

Area 1: Red square (C)

Areas 2, 3, 4 and 5: 1 set of 4 matching brown triangles (D)

BOTTOM ROW BLOCKS

1. Note that each Maple Leaf block is comprised of 3 units. When working on a block, make sure the brown background prints (G and H) match and the leaf's red or orange prints (E and F) match. Paper piece each Maple Leaf unit, covering the areas in numerical order as follows:

Area 1: Light brown rectangle (I)

Areas 2, 3, 6, 7, 11, and 13: Brown triangles (H)

Areas 4, 9, and 10: Red or orange squares (E)

Areas 5, 8, 12, and 14: Red or orange triangles (F)

Area 15: Brown square (G)

2. Join the 3 units as shown to make a Maple Leaf block. Gently remove the paper from behind the block and press the seam allowances open. Repeat to make 3 Maple Leaf blocks—2 red and 1 orange. *fig. C*

A. Flying Geese unit

B. Square-in-a-Square

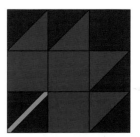

C. Maple Leaf block

hello fall pillow

Say "Hello!" to fall with this inviting pillow. A rainbow of fall-colored patchwork is the perfect accompaniment to the wool leaf and acorn appliqués inspired by the big oak tree in our front yard.

Materials

Cotton yardage is based on 40˝-wide fabric. Wool sizes are for felted wool.

FABRICS

Assorted fall prints: 1 mini charm square pack *or* 42 squares 2½˝ × 2½˝ (I used Sweet Pea by Kansas Troubles Quilters.)

Dark blue print: ½ yard for pillow backing

Lining fabric: ½ yard of muslin

Tan solid: 5˝ × 7˝ for pillow inset

FELTED WOOL

Rust: 4˝ × 4˝ for oak leaf

Medium brown: 2˝ × 3˝ for acorns

Dark brown textured: 2˝ × 2˝ for acorn caps

EMBROIDERY FLOSS

Colors to match wool

Rust perle cotton #8

Tan for swirls

OTHER SUPPLIES

Batting: 16˝ × 20˝

Pillow form: 12˝ × 16˝

Freezer paper

Water-soluble fabric marking pen

Cutting

ASSORTED FALL PRINTS

• Cut 42 squares 2½˝ × 2½˝ if you've chosen not to use a mini charm square pack.

DARK BLUE PRINT

• Cut 2 backing panels 12˝ × 12½˝.

LINING FABRIC

• Cut 1 rectangle 16˝ × 20˝.

TAN SOLID

• Cut 1 rectangle 5˝ × 7˝.

Making the Pillow Top

Use a ¼˝ seam allowance. Follow the pressing arrows provided in the diagram(s). For more information about pressing seam allowances, see Pressing Matters (page 19).

PILLOW INSET APPLIQUÉ

Refer to Freezer-Paper Method (page 108) for step-by-step instructions. Refer to Stitching Wool Appliqués (page 109) as needed.

1. Use the Hello Fall Pillow appliqué patterns (page 62) to prepare the wool appliqués.

2. With a water-soluble marking pen, draw a 4½˝ × 6½˝ rectangle centered on the tan rectangle. This rectangle is the appliqué placement area, *including* the ¼˝ seam allowance, and will be the trim size after the appliqué has been completed. (The finished size will measure 4˝ × 6˝.)

3. Use the project photo close-up as a guide to position the wool appliqués within the drawn rectangle of the inset. Pin.

4. Blanket stitch the oak leaf in place with *rust perle cotton #8*. Use the same perle cotton and a running stitch to stitch veins on the leaf.

5. Whipstitch the remaining appliqués in place using *1 strand* of embroidery floss that matches the wool.

6. Trim the pillow inset to 4½˝ × 6½˝ using the lines you marked in Step 2.

PILLOW TOP ASSEMBLY

1. Lay out the appliquéd pillow inset and the 42 squares as shown.

2. When you are happy with the arrangement, join the squares into rows; then join the rows.

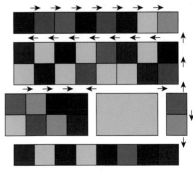

Pillow top assembly

EMBROIDERY

Refer to Embroidery Basics (page 110) for detailed information. Use *2 strands* of embroidery floss for all embroidery.

1. With the water-soluble fabric marking pen, use the Hello Fall Pillow embroidery pattern (below right) to mark the lettering and the Hello Fall Pillow oak leaf appliqué pattern (below) to mark the swirls onto the pillow inset. A lightbox or other light source is helpful.

2. Layer the pillow top, batting, and lining fabric. Baste.

3. Backstitch the lettering on the pillow inset using *dark brown* floss.

4. Backstitch the swirling marked lines through all layers using *tan* floss.

QUILTING

1. Quilt the pillow top as desired. The featured pillow was machine quilted ¼˝ along both sides of each seam, stopping or starting at the inset as necessary and knotting the thread ends at the back (lining side) of the pillow top.

2. Trim the batting and lining even with the pillow top.

Finishing the Pillow

1. To make the pillow back, hem one of the 12½˝ edges of each backing panel. To do this, fold the edge toward the wrong side ⅜˝ and then ⅜˝ again, and press.

2. Stitch close to the inside folded edge.

3. Layer one backing panel on the pillow top, right sides together and raw edges aligned.

4. Layer the remaining panel on the opposite side of the pillow top, right sides together and raw edges aligned. Pin.

5. Stitch around all the edges and through all the layers with a ¼˝ seam.

6. Trim the corners to reduce bulk, turn the pillow right side out, and insert the pillow form.

Pillow assembly

---

hello fall pillow

Appliqué Patterns

Cut 1 of each except where noted.

Embroidery Pattern

FALL

Pillow lettering

Oak leaf

Acorn: Cut 2.

Acorn cap: Cut 2.

fly south mini quilt

Sawtooth Stars and paper-pieced Flying Geese surround a center medallion of maple leaves.
This little quilt is an ode to one of my favorite fall color palettes—rusty orange, brown, and slate blue.
The wide binding on this quilt does double duty as a narrow outer border.

Materials

Cotton yardage is based on 40″-wide fabric. This pattern is scrap or precut friendly, though an entire precut pack is not required. Precut sizes shown in the materials list indicate scrap sizes as well.

FABRICS

Blue prints: 4 assorted fat eighths 9″ × 22″ for backgrounds

5 assorted charm squares 5″ × 5″ of *additional* blue prints for Flying Geese borders

Rust prints: 4 assorted precut 10″ squares *or* 4 assorted scraps at least 6″ × 6″ for Maple Leaf blocks

4 assorted charm squares 5″ × 5″ for Sawtooth Star blocks and Flying Geese borders

20 assorted mini charm squares 2½″ × 2½″ for Flying Geese borders

Brown prints: ⅓ yard for wide binding

5 assorted charm squares 5″ × 5″ for Sawtooth Star blocks and Flying Geese borders

12 assorted mini charm squares 2½″ × 2½″ for Flying Geese borders

Backing: 1 fat quarter

OTHER SUPPLIES

Batting: 18″ × 18″

Foundation paper for paper piecing

pumpkin spice table runner

Formations of Flying Geese in spicy shades of red, orange, and plum share space with warm wool leaves and ripe berries. Plum might seem like an unexpected color for fall, but if you look closely, you can see shades of purple everywhere in the New England fall landscape.

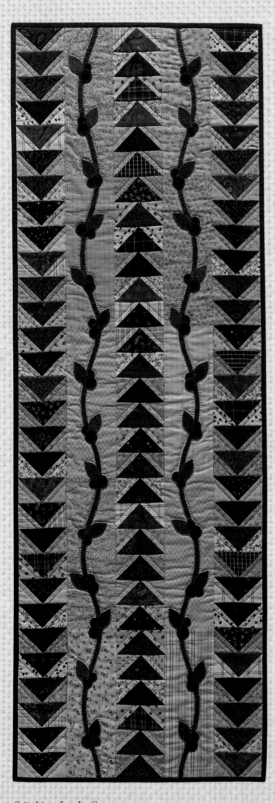

Materials

Cotton yardage is based on 40˝-wide fabric. Wool sizes are for felted wool. This pattern is scrap or precut friendly, though an entire precut pack is not required. Precut sizes shown in the materials list indicate scrap sizes as well. Optional: Binding may be cut on the length of fabric (LOF) from the backing fabric if you choose to have a matching back and binding.

FABRIC

Tan prints: 5 assorted fat eighths 9˝ × 22˝ for background rows

12 assorted precut 10˝ squares for Flying Geese backgrounds

Orange prints: 7 assorted charm squares 5˝ × 5˝ for Flying Geese

Red prints: 8 assorted charm squares 5˝ × 5˝ for Flying Geese

Plum prints: ⅓ yard for binding (*optional*)

8 assorted charm squares 5˝ × 5˝ for Flying Geese

Backing: 1¾ yards (*Optional:* Cut the binding from this fabric.)

FELTED WOOL

Brown: 5˝ × 11˝ for vines

Assorted brown: 4 squares 5˝ × 5˝ for leaves

Assorted red: 4 squares 3˝ × 3˝ for berries

Assorted purple: 2 squares 5˝ × 5˝ for berries

EMBROIDERY FLOSS

Tan

OTHER SUPPLIES

Batting: 26˝ × 61˝

Freezer paper

Cutting

TAN PRINTS

From each *assorted fat eighth, cut:*

• 2 rectangles 4″ × 11″ for the background rows

From each *assorted precut 10″ square, cut:*

• 8 squares 2⅝″ × 2⅝″ for the Flying Geese backgrounds

ORANGE PRINTS

From each *assorted charm square, cut:*

• 1 square 4¾″ × 4¾″ for the Flying Geese

RED PRINTS

From each *assorted charm square, cut:*

• 1 square 4¾″ × 4¾″ for the Flying Geese

PLUM PRINTS

From yardage, cut:

• 4 strips 2¼″ × width of fabric (WOF) for binding *or* 3 strips LOF from backing fabric (*optional*)

From each *assorted charm square, cut:*

• 1 square 4¾″ × 4¾″ for the Flying Geese

BROWN WOOL

• Cut 12 strips ⅜″ × 11″ for the vines.

Making the Flying Geese Blocks

Use a ¼″ seam allowance. Follow the pressing arrows provided in the diagram(s). For more information about pressing seam allowances, see Pressing Matters (page 19).

1. Use a pencil to lightly draw a diagonal line from corner to corner on the wrong side of 4 matching 2⅝″ tan squares (Flying Geese backgrounds).

2. Layer 2 marked background squares atop a 4¾″ orange, red, or plum square, right sides together and marked lines positioned as shown. Sew a scant ¼″ from each side of the drawn lines. *fig. A*

3. Cut between the rows of stitching along the drawn lines. Press as shown. *figs. B & C*

4. Place 1 additional marked background square atop each of the 2 units, right sides together as shown. Sew a scant ¼″ from each side of the drawn lines. *fig. D*

5. Cut between the rows of stitching along the drawn lines for both units. *fig. E*

6. Trim the 4 Flying Geese to 2¼″ × 4″.

7. Repeat with the remaining background squares and 4¾″ orange, red, and plum squares to make the required 90 Flying Geese blocks. *fig. F*

A.

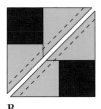

B.

C.

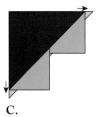

D.

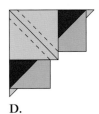

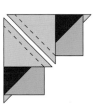

E.

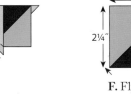

F. Flying Geese block

Assembling the Table Runner

1. Lay out 30 Flying Geese blocks and sew them together in a row, all pointing in the same direction. Press the seam allowances away from the Flying Geese points. Make 3 rows of Flying Geese.

2. Join 5 tan 11″ rectangles end to end (varying prints) to make a background row. Press the seam allowances open. Make 2 background rows.

3. Join the 5 rows, alternating Flying Geese and background rows. Note that the Flying Geese in the center row point in the opposite direction of the Flying Geese in the outermost rows. Press the seam allowances toward the background rows.

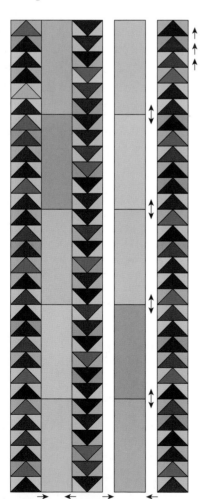

Table runner assembly

Appliquéing the Table Runner

Refer to Freezer-Paper Method (page 108) for step-by-step instructions. Refer to Stitching Wool Appliqués (page 109) as needed. Use *1 strand* of *tan* embroidery floss for all appliqué.

1. Use the Pumpkin Spice Table Runner appliqué patterns (below right) to prepare the wool appliqués.

2. Use the project photo as a guide to arrange the brown wool strips on the background rows of the table runner in a manner resembling a vine. As you arrange the vine, note that wherever 2 strips meet, the junction should later be covered by a leaf or a berry. When you are satisfied with your arrangement, pin and whipstitch the vine in place.

3. Position the remaining wool appliqués on the background rows as desired. Make sure that all vine junctions are covered by either a leaf or a berry. Pin. Whipstitch the wool appliqués in place.

Finishing the Table Runner

1. Layer the appliquéd table runner top, batting, and backing. *(If you are cutting the binding and backing from the same yardage, cut along the length of fabric [LOF].)* Baste.

2. Quilt as desired. The featured quilt shows tan quilting thread used to hand quilt ¼″ outside each of the Flying Geese and alongside the wool appliqués.

3. Bind the table runner using the plum binding strips. (Find additional information about binding a quilt at ctpub.com/quilting-sewing-tips.)

----

pumpkin spice table runner
Appliqué Patterns

Leaf: Cut 28.

Large berry: Cut 24 (12 red/12 purple).

Small berry: Cut 32 (16 red/16 purple).

harvest skies quilt

Bright sunflowers and red and orange maple leaves dance against a backdrop
of brilliant blue skies. This cozy lap quilt is perfect for crisp fall days.

Machine quilted by
Joyce Lundrigan

Materials

Cotton yardage is based on 40˝-wide fabric. This pattern is scrap or precut friendly, though an entire precut pack is not required.
Precut sizes shown in the materials list indicate scrap sizes as well.

FABRIC

Blue print: 3⅜ yards for background

Second blue print: ½ yard for binding

Red prints: 9 assorted fat eighths 9˝ × 22˝ for Maple Leaf blocks

Orange prints: 9 assorted fat eighths 9˝ × 22˝ for Maple Leaf blocks

Gold prints: 5 assorted precut 10˝ squares for Sawtooth Star blocks

Brown prints: 25 assorted mini charm squares 2½˝ × 2½˝ or 7 assorted charm squares 5˝ × 5˝ for Sawtooth Star blocks

Second brown print: 1 fat eighth 9˝ × 22˝ for Maple Leaf block stems

Backing: 4 yards

OTHER SUPPLIES

Batting: 69˝ × 69˝

Foundation paper for paper piecing

Cutting

BLUE PRINT

Cut the blue print yardage exactly *in the following order.*

From the crosswise grain/width *(WOF) of fabric, cut:*

- 8 strips 6½″ × WOF. Crosscut into:

  60 sashing rectangles 4½″ × 6½″

From the lengthwise grain *(LOF) of the remaining blue print fabric, cut:*

- 2 border strips 2½″ × 56½″
- 2 border strips 2½″ × 60½″

From the remaining 30″ width (WOF) of the blue print fabric, cut:

- 4 strips 6″ × WOF. Crosscut into:

  18 background squares 6″ × 6″ for the Maple Leaf blocks

- 7 strips 3¼″ × WOF. Crosscut into:

  61 squares 3¼″ × 3¼″

    Set aside 25 of the 61 background squares for the Sawtooth Star Flying Geese.

    Cut each of the remaining 36 squares in half diagonally once to yield 2 background triangles for the paper-pieced Maple Leaf stem units (B).

- 3 strips 2½″ × WOF. Crosscut into:

  36 squares 2½″ × 2½″ for the Maple Leaf background corners

- 5 strips 1½″ × WOF. Crosscut into:

  100 squares 1½″ × 1½″ for the Sawtooth Star background corners

SECOND BLUE PRINT

- Cut 7 strips 2¼″ × WOF for the binding.

RED PRINTS

From each of the 9 assorted fat eighths, cut:

- 1 square 6″ × 6″ for the Maple Leaf blocks
- 6 squares 2½″ × 2½″ for the Maple Leaf blocks

ORANGE PRINTS

From each of the 9 assorted fat eighths, cut:

- 1 square 6″ × 6″ for the Maple Leaf blocks
- 6 squares 2½″ × 2½″ for the Maple Leaf blocks

GOLD PRINTS

From each of the 5 assorted precut 10″ squares, cut:

- 20 squares 1⅞″ × 1⅞″ for the Sawtooth Star Flying Geese

    Sort the squares into 25 sets of 4 matching squares each.

BROWN PRINTS

From each of the 7 assorted charm squares, cut:

- 4 squares 2½″ × 2½″ for the Sawtooth Star centers if you choose not to use mini charm squares

SECOND BROWN PRINT

- Cut 36 rectangles 1″ × 4″ for the Maple Leaf stem units (A).

Making the Maple Leaf Blocks

Use a ¼˝ seam allowance. Follow the pressing arrows provided in the diagram(s). For more information about pressing seam allowances, see Pressing Matters (page 19).

MAPLE LEAF STEMS

Photocopy or download and print the project patterns (see Foundation Paper-Piecing Patterns, page 10).

1. Make 6 copies of the Harvest Skies Quilt foundation pattern (page 76) onto foundation paper. Cut out each pattern ¼˝ beyond its outer dashed line. Refer to Paper-Piecing Basics (page 105) for step-by-step instructions.

2. Paper piece 36 Maple Leaf stem units *(fig. A)*, covering the areas in numerical order. Use the pieces designated for each area as follows:

A. Maple Leaf stem unit

   Area 1: Brown stem rectangle (A)

   Areas 2 and 3: Blue background triangle (B)

HALF-SQUARE TRIANGLES

1. On the wrong side of a 6˝ red or orange square, use a pencil to lightly draw 2 diagonal lines from corner to corner, and 1 horizontal and 1 vertical line through the center of the block.

2. Layer the marked square atop a 6˝ blue background square, right sides together. Sew a scant ¼˝ from each side of the diagonal lines. *fig. B*

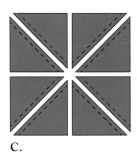

B.   **C.**

3. Cut the pair apart on all drawn lines to make 8 half-square triangles. *fig. C*

4. Press the half-square triangles open. Trim to measure 2½˝ × 2½˝.

5. Repeat Steps 1–4, pairing the remaining 6˝ red and orange squares with 6˝ blue background squares. Sort the half-square triangles into 36 sets of 4 matching half-square triangles each. *fig. D*

D. Maple Leaf half-square triangle

MAPLE LEAF BLOCK ASSEMBLY

1. Select a set of half-square triangles, 3 red or orange 2½˝ squares that match the set of half-square triangles, 1 blue 2½˝ corner square, and 1 Maple Leaf stem unit. Lay out the pieces in 3 horizontal rows, as shown.

2. Join the pieces in each row.

3. Join the rows. Gently remove the paper from behind the stem unit.

4. Repeat Steps 1–3 to make 36 Maple Leaf blocks, measuring 6½˝ × 6½˝. *fig. E*

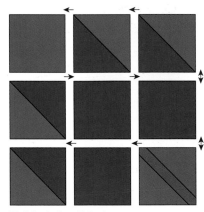

E. Maple Leaf block

Making the Sawtooth Star Blocks

FLYING GEESE UNITS

1. Use a pencil to lightly draw a diagonal line from corner to corner on the wrong side of a set of gold Flying Geese squares.

2. Layer 2 marked gold squares atop a 3¼″ blue background square, right sides together and marked lines positioned as shown. Sew a scant ¼″ from each side of the drawn lines. *fig. A*

3. Cut between the rows of stitching along the drawn lines. Press as shown. *figs. B & C*

4. Place 1 additional marked gold square atop each of the 2 units, right sides together as shown. Sew a scant ¼″ from each side of the drawn lines. *fig. D*

5. Cut between the rows of stitching along the drawn lines for both units. *fig. E*

6. Trim the 4 Flying Geese units to 1½″ × 2½″. Keep these together as 1 set to use in a Sawtooth Star block. Repeat Steps 1–5 using the remaining 24 blue 3¼″ background squares and 24 sets of gold Flying Geese squares. *fig. F*

SAWTOOTH STAR BLOCK ASSEMBLY

1. Sew 2 Flying Geese units from a matched set of 4 to opposite sides of 1 brown 2½″ center square, making a center row.

2. Sew a 1½″ blue background square to both ends of the remaining 2 Flying Geese units, making 2 Flying Geese rows.

3. Join the 2 Flying Geese rows to the top and bottom of the center row as shown to complete the Sawtooth Star block.

4. Repeat Steps 1–3 to make 25 Sawtooth Star blocks, measuring 4½″ × 4½″. *fig. G*

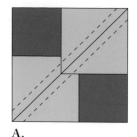

A.

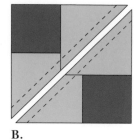

B.

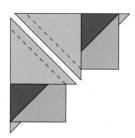

C.

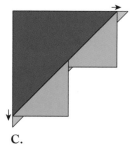

D.

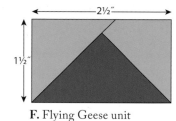

E.

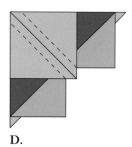

F. Flying Geese unit

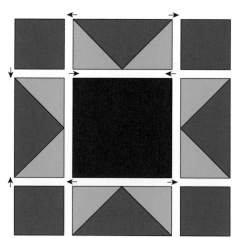

G. Sawtooth Star block

Assembling the Quilt

1. Lay out 6 Maple Leaf blocks and 5 blue sashing rectangles in alternating positions. Notice how the direction of the maple leaves changes with every second block. Join the blocks and sashing to make a row. Make 6 Maple Leaf rows. Note that 3 of the 6 rows are the same as the original layout, just turned 180°.

2. Lay out 6 sashing rectangles and 5 Sawtooth Star blocks in alternating positions. Join the sashing and blocks to make a Sawtooth Star row. Make 5 Sawtooth Star rows.

3. Lay out 6 Maple Leaf rows and 5 Sawtooth Star rows in alternating positions, paying attention to the direction of the maple leaves from row to row. Join the rows. Press the seam allowances open.

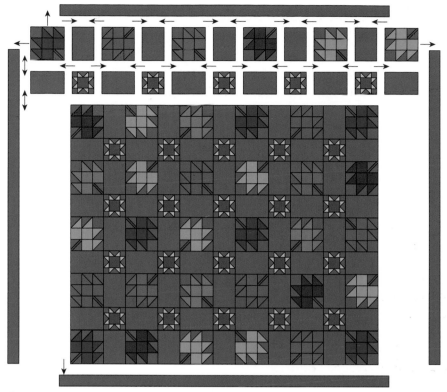

Quilt assembly

4. Matching the centers, sew a 56½˝ blue border strip to the left and right sides of the quilt.

5. Matching the centers, sew a 60½˝ blue border strip to the top and bottom of the quilt.

Finishing the Quilt

1. Layer the quilt top, batting, and backing. Baste.

2. Quilt as desired. The featured quilt was machine quilted with a diagonal crosshatch.

3. Bind the quilt using the strips from the second blue print. (Find additional information about binding a quilt at ctpub.com/quilting-sewing-tips.)

harvest skies quilt

Foundation Pattern

Photocopy this page 6 times onto foundation paper to make 36 stem units.

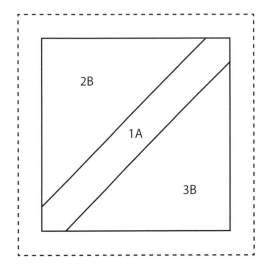

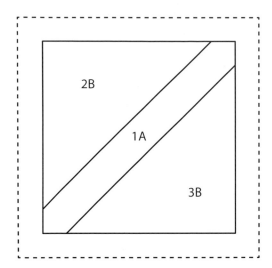

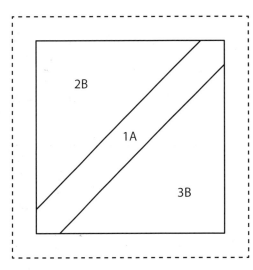

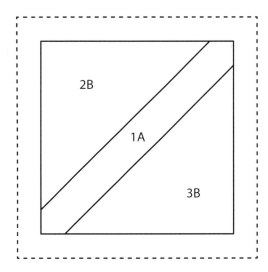

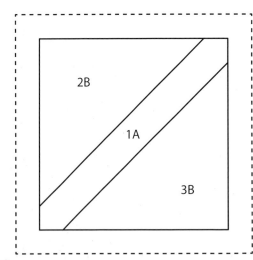

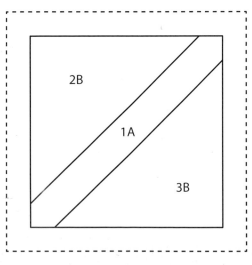

Maple Leaf stem units

winter

Winter in New England is magical. Whether it brings softly falling flurries, blustery winds and swirling snow, or crystal-clear skies, it's always beautiful. And after spending a chilly day outside making snowmen, skiing, or snowshoeing, there's nothing like returning home, pink-cheeked, for a cozy evening spent by the fire.

little house—winter wallhanging

After a long winter's nap at Little House, a bright-red cardinal and a carefully crafted snowman are the first to greet a sparkling new day.

Materials

Cotton yardage is based on 40″-wide fabric. Wool sizes are for felted wool. This pattern is scrap or precut friendly, though an entire precut pack or roll is not required. Precut sizes shown in the materials list indicate scrap sizes as well.

FABRICS

Medium blue print: 1 precut 10″ square for appliqué background

Dark blue prints: ⅛ yard for single-fold binding

4 assorted precut 2½″ strips at least 9″ long for quilt-center borders

4 assorted charm squares 5″ × 5″ for Shoo Fly and Square-in-a-Square backgrounds

10 assorted mini charm squares 2½″ × 2½″ for Flying Geese backgrounds and bottom row sashing

White print: 1 precut 10″ square for Shoo Fly blocks

Light blue prints: 5 assorted mini charm squares 2½″ × 2½″ for top row blocks

Red prints: 4 assorted mini charm squares 2½″ × 2½″ for Flying Geese

Backing: 1 fat quarter *or* 1 rectangle 12″ × 16″

FELTED WOOL

White: 2″ × 9″ for snow and snowman

Dark red: 3″ × 5″ for house

Textured dark brown: 2″ × 4″ for roof

Medium brown: 2″ × 4″ for tree

Dark brown: 2″ × 2″ for windows

Dark gold: 2″ × 2″ for door and chimney

EMBROIDERY FLOSS

Colors to match wool

Gray for smoke

Red for wreath

Black and orange for snowman

Green perle cotton #8 for wreath and scarf

OTHER SUPPLIES

Batting: 12″ × 16″

Lightweight paper-backed fusible web (17″ wide): ¼ yard

Foundation paper for paper piecing

Small bird button (I used the Tiny Mr. Cardinal from Just Another Button Company.)

Water-soluble fabric marking pen

Cutting

MEDIUM BLUE PRINT

- Cut 1 square 8″ × 8″ for the appliqué center.

DARK BLUE PRINTS

From yardage, cut:

- 2 strips 1¼″ × width of fabric (WOF) for the binding

From 4 assorted precut 2½″ strips, cut the quilt-center borders:

- 2 strips 1¼″ × 8″
- 2 strips 1¼″ × 6½″

From each of 3 assorted charm squares, cut 1 set of:

- 2 squares 2¼″ × 2¼″, each cut in half diagonally once to make 4 triangles (G)
- 4 rectangles 1¼″ × 1½″ (H)

From 1 charm square, cut 1 set of:

- 2 squares 2¼″ × 2¼″, each cut in half diagonally once to make 4 matching print triangles (D)

From 10 assorted mini charm squares, cut:

- 2 assorted rectangles 1¼″ × 2½″ for the bottom row sashing
- 8 squares 2¼″ × 2¼″, each cut in half diagonally once to make 8 triangle *pairs* (B)

WHITE PRINT

From 1 precut 10″ square, cut:

- 6 squares 2¼″ × 2¼″, each cut in half diagonally once to make 12 triangles (E)
- 3 squares 1¼″ × 1¼″ (F)

LIGHT BLUE PRINTS

From 5 assorted mini charm squares, cut:

- 4 rectangles 1½″ × 2½″ (A)
- 1 square 1¾″ × 1¾″ (C)

RED PRINTS

From 4 assorted mini charm squares, cut:

- 4 rectangles 1½″ × 2½″ (A)

The Quilt Center

Because of the small pieces and the narrow, sharp points of the tree branches, the fusible web method for wool appliqué is suggested for this project. Refer to Fusible Web Method (page 109) for step-by-step instructions. Refer to Stitching Wool Appliqués (page 109) as needed.

APPLIQUÉ

1. Use the general Little House Wallhanging appliqué patterns (page 13) for the house, roof, windows, door, chimney, tree, and snow, and the Little House—Winter Wallhanging appliqué pattern (page 82) for the snowman to prepare the wool appliqués.

2. In the center of the medium blue fabric, draw a 6½″ × 6½″ square with a water-soluble marking pen. This square is the appliqué placement area, *including* the ¼″ seam allowance, and will be the trim size after the appliqué and embroidery have been completed. (The finished size will measure 6″ × 6″.)

3. Use the project photo as a guide to position the wool appliqués within the drawn square. Make sure that the house is centered from left to right and that the snow will be enclosed within the seams of the finished project.

Note: Certain appliqué pieces overlap, so be sure to tuck the bottom layer of pieces under the top layers before fusing. For example, the snow overlaps the bottom edges of the house and door.

4. Once you are satisfied with the placement of the wool appliqués, fuse the pieces to the background.

5. Whipstitch the wool appliqués in place using *1 strand* of embroidery floss. Use *gold* floss for the house and windows and *dark brown* floss for the door. For the remaining appliqués, match the floss to the wool. It isn't necessary to whipstitch the bottom and side edges of the snow because they'll be enclosed within the seams of the finished project.

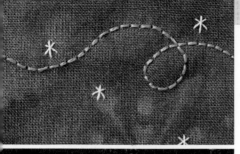

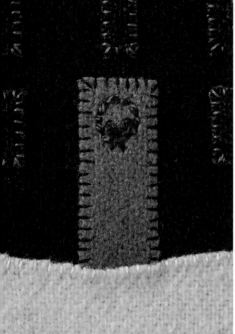

EMBROIDERY

Refer to Embroidery Basics (page 110) for detailed information. Use *2 strands* of floss for all embroidery unless otherwise indicated.

1. Trace the dashed lines of the tree branches (see the Little House Wallhanging appliqué patterns, page 13) onto the fabric using the water-soluble fabric marking pen.

2. Backstitch the tree branches using *medium brown* floss.

3. Freehand draw and then backstitch a curving line of smoke rising from the chimney using *gray* floss.

4. Use *1 strand* of *green perle cotton #8* and a tiny backstitch for the wreath on the door. Use a length of the *green perle cotton #8* to make a scarf on the snowman by running the floss behind the snowman's neck and knotting the strands in front.

5. Stitch 2 tiny lazy daisies and 2 straight stitches using *red* floss for the bow on the bottom of the wreath.

6. Using *1 strand* of *black* floss for the snowman's eyes and *1 strand* of *orange* floss for the snowman's nose, stitch tiny French knots. Backstitch the snowman's mouth with *1 strand* of *black* floss.

7. Stitch multiple snowflakes using *white* floss and 3 straight stitches in the shape of a star.

TRIMMING

Trim the appliquéd and embroidered quilt center to 6½˝ × 6½˝ along the marked lines you drew on the fabric previously.

Making the Paper-Pieced Blocks

Photocopy or download and print the project patterns (see Foundation Paper-Piecing Patterns, page 10).

Copy the Little House Wallhanging top row foundation patterns (page 12) and Little House—Winter Wallhanging bottom row foundation patterns (page 82) onto foundation paper. Cut out each pattern ¼˝ beyond its outer dashed line. Refer to Paper-Piecing Basics (page 105) for step-by-step instructions.

TOP ROW BLOCKS

1. Paper piece 2 Flying Geese units *(fig. A)*, covering the areas in numerical order. Use the pieces designated for each area as follows:

Areas 1 and 7: Light blue rectangles (A)

Areas 2 and 3, 5 and 6, 8 and 9, 11 and 12: Dark-blue triangle pairs (B)

Areas 4 and 10: Red rectangles (A)

2. Paper piece 1 Square-in-a-Square block *(fig. B)*, covering the areas in numerical order. Use the pieces designated for each area as follows:

Area 1: Light blue square (C)

Areas 2, 3, 4, and 5: 1 set of 4 matching dark blue triangles (D)

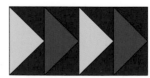

A. Flying Geese unit

B. Square-in-a-Square

BOTTOM ROW BLOCKS

1. Note that each Shoo Fly block is comprised of 3 units. Paper piece a Shoo Fly block, covering the areas in numerical order. When working on a block, make sure the dark blue prints (G and H) match. Use the pieces designated for each area as follows:

Areas 1, 5, 9, and 13: Dark blue triangles (G)   **Areas 3, 6, 8, and 11:** Dark blue rectangles (H)

Areas 2, 4, 10, and 12: White triangles (E)   **Area 7:** White print square (F)

C. Shoo Fly block

2. Join the 3 units to make a Shoo Fly block. Gently remove the paper from behind the block and press the seam allowances open. Repeat to make 3 Shoo Fly blocks. *fig. C*

Assembling the Quilt

Use a ¼˝ seam allowance. Follow the pressing arrows provided in the diagram(s). For more information about pressing seam allowances, see Pressing Matters (page 19).

1. Sew the 2 dark-blue 6½˝ quilt-center border strips to the right and left sides of the trimmed quilt center.

2. Sew the 2 remaining dark-blue quilt-center border strips to the top and bottom to finish the framed quilt center.

3. Lay out 2 Flying Geese units and position the Square-in-a-Square block between them. The Flying Geese should point toward the center. Join the pieces. Gently remove the paper from behind the blocks and press the seam allowances open to complete the top row.

4. Lay out 3 Shoo Fly blocks and 2 dark-blue bottom-row sashing rectangles in alternating positions. Join the pieces to complete the bottom row.

5. Lay out the top row, framed quilt center, and bottom row as shown. Join the rows and quilt center.

Quilt assembly

Finishing the Quilt

1. Referring to the project photo, stitch the small bird button to the tree.

2. Layer the quilt top, batting, and backing. If desired, baste and quilt the layers. (Because of the small size of the project, quilting is not necessary.)

3. If desired, prepare and stitch a hanging sleeve to the back of the quilt. Refer to Adding a Hanging Sleeve to a Small Quilt (page 104) for step-by-step instructions.

4. Bind the quilt. Refer to Single-Fold Binding (page 104) for step-by-step binding instructions.

little house—winter wallhanging

Bottom Row Foundation Patterns

Photocopy this page once onto foundation paper.

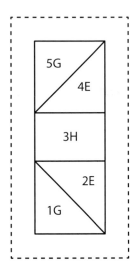
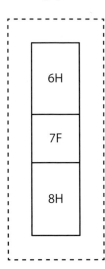
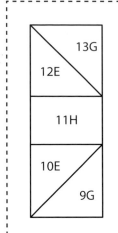

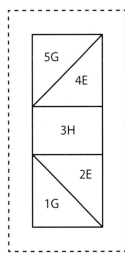
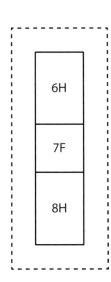
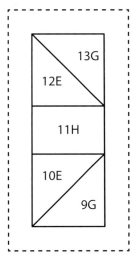

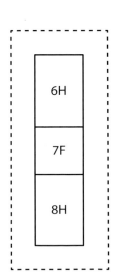
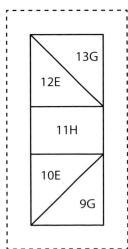
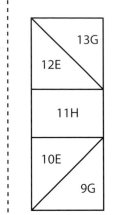

Appliqué Pattern

Pattern is reversed for fusible web appliqué. Cut 1.

Snowman

welcome winter pillow

Bundled up against the chill, a charming wool snowman poses amid sweet embroidered snowflakes.
This cozy pillow welcomes winter perfectly.

Materials

Cotton yardage is based on 40˝-wide fabric. Wool sizes are for felted wool.

FABRICS

Assorted winter prints: 1 mini charm square pack *or* 42 squares 2½˝ × 2½˝ (I used Snowman Gatherings by Primitive Gatherings.)

Dark blue print: ½ yard for pillow backing

Lining fabric: ½ yard of muslin

Tan solid: 5˝ × 7˝ for pillow inset

White print: 2˝ × 6˝ for snow

Medium blue homespun: Long scrap for scarf

FELTED WOOL

White: 3˝ × 5˝ for snowman

Dark blue textured: 2˝ × 2˝ for hat

EMBROIDERY FLOSS

Colors to match wool

Black

Orange

Brown

White perle cotton #12

OTHER SUPPLIES

Batting: 16˝ × 20˝

Pillow form: 12˝ × 16˝

Lightweight paper-backed fusible web: 2˝ × 7˝

Freezer paper

Water-soluble fabric marking pen

Cutting

ASSORTED WINTER PRINTS

- Cut 42 squares 2½″ × 2½″ if you've chosen not to use a mini charm square pack.

DARK BLUE PRINT

- Cut 2 backing panels 12″ × 12½″.

LINING FABRIC

- Cut 1 rectangle 16″ × 20″.

TAN SOLID

- Cut 1 rectangle 5″ × 7″.

MEDIUM BLUE HOMESPUN

- Cut 1 strip ¼″ × 8″.

Making the Pillow Top

Use a ¼″ seam allowance. Follow the pressing arrows provided in the diagram(s). For more information about pressing seam allowances, see Pressing Matters (page 19).

PILLOW INSET APPLIQUÉ

In this project, two appliqué methods will be used. Refer to Freezer-Paper Method (page 108) and Fusible Web Method (page 109) for step-by-step instructions and to Stitching Wool Appliqués (page 109) as needed.

1. Prepare the wool appliqués (all except the snow) using the Welcome Winter Pillow appliqué patterns (page 86) and freezer paper.

2. Trace the snow pattern (page 86) onto the paper side of lightweight fusible web. Cut out the snow shape roughly ¼″ outside the drawn lines.

3. Following the manufacturer's instructions, fuse the snow shape, fusible web side down, to the wrong side of the white print fabric. Cut out the white snow shape exactly on the drawn lines and remove the backing paper. Set aside until later.

4. With a water-soluble marking pen, draw a 4½″ × 6½″ rectangle centered on the tan rectangle. This rectangle is the appliqué placement area, *including* the ¼″ seam allowance, and will be the trim size after the appliqué has been completed. (The finished size will measure 4″ × 6″.)

5. Use the project photo close-up as a guide to position the wool appliqués within the drawn rectangle of the inset. Pin.

6. Before stitching, wrap the medium-blue homespun strip around the snowman's neck, centering it.

7. Whipstitch the snowman, hat, and brim in place using *1 strand* of embroidery floss that matches the wool.

8. Knot the snowman's scarf and trim as desired.

9. Position the snow shape so that it overlaps the bottom edge of the snowman. The side and bottom edges of the snow shape should overlap the marked rectangle lines so that they will be enclosed within the seams of the finished project. Fuse the snow to the background.

10. Blanket stitch the top edge of the snow using *white perle cotton #12*.

11. Trim the pillow inset to 4½″ × 6½″ using the lines you marked in Step 4.

PILLOW TOP ASSEMBLY

1. Lay out the appliquéd pillow inset and the 42 squares as shown.

2. When you are happy with the arrangement, join the squares into rows; then join the rows.

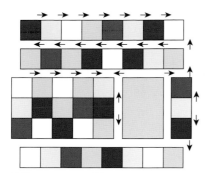

Pillow top assembly

EMBROIDERY

Refer to Embroidery Basics (page 110) for detailed information. Use *2 strands* of embroidery floss for all embroidery unless otherwise indicated.

1. Use the Welcome Winter Pillow embroidery pattern (page 86) to mark the lettering on the pillow inset with the water-soluble fabric marking pen. A lightbox or other light source is helpful.

2. Stitch French knots for the snowman's eyes and buttons using *black* floss. Use *1 strand* of *black* floss and a tiny backstitch to stitch the snowman's mouth.

3. Take several long straight stiches using *orange* floss to make the snowman's nose.

4. Backstitch the snowman's arms using *brown* floss.

5. Layer the pillow top, batting, and lining fabric. Baste.

6. Backstitch the lettering on the pillow inset through all layers using *white* floss.

7. Stitch 3 straight stitches in the shape of a star for each snowflake using *1 strand* of *white perle cotton #12*.

QUILTING

1. Quilt the pillow top as desired. The featured pillow was machine quilted ¼˝ along both sides of each seam, stopping or starting at the inset as necessary and knotting the thread ends at the back (lining side) of the pillow top.

2. Trim the batting and lining even with the pillow top.

Finishing the Pillow

1. To make the pillow back, hem one of the 12½˝ edges of each backing panel. To do this, fold the edge toward the wrong side ⅜˝ and then ⅜˝ again, and press.

2. Stitch close to the inside folded edge.

3. Layer one backing panel on the pillow top, right sides together and raw edges aligned.

4. Layer the remaining panel on the opposite side of the pillow top, right sides together and raw edges aligned. Pin.

5. Stitch around all the edges and through all the layers with a ¼˝ seam.

6. Trim the corners to reduce bulk, turn the pillow right side out, and insert the pillow form.

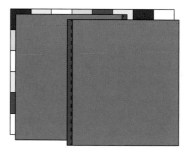

Pillow assembly

welcome winter pillow

Appliqué Patterns

Cut 1 of each.

Hat

Brim

Snowman

Snow (reversed for fusible appliqué)

Embroidery Pattern

Pillow lettering

north star mini quilt

Winter-white stars and an embroidered snowflake sparkle against a darkening blue background. This little quilt celebrates the beauty of a silent winter's night.

Materials

Cotton yardage is based on 40˝-wide fabric. This pattern is scrap or precut friendly, though an entire precut pack or roll is not required. Precut sizes shown in the materials list indicate scrap sizes as well.

FABRICS

Dark blue print: ½ yard for background, borders, and binding

Light blue print: 1 fat eighth 9˝ × 22˝ for center and background

Ivory prints: 8 assorted squares for blocks, either precut 10˝ squares *or* scraps at least 6˝ × 6˝

Backing: 1 fat quarter *or* ½ yard

EMBROIDERY THREAD

Ivory perle cotton #12

OTHER SUPPLIES

Batting: 18˝ × 18˝

Water-soluble fabric marking pen

Cutting

DARK BLUE PRINT

- Cut 2 strips 2¼″ × width of fabric (WOF) for the binding.

- Cut 1 strip 2″ × WOF. Crosscut into:

  8 squares 2″ × 2″ for the half-square triangles

- Cut 4 strips 1½″ × WOF. Crosscut into:

  2 strips 1½″ × 14½″ for the border

  2 strips 1½″ × 12½″ for the border

  12 rectangles 1½″ × 2½″ for the Flying Geese

  20 squares 1½″ × 1½″ for the block corners

LIGHT BLUE PRINT

- Cut 1 square 4½″ × 4½″ for the quilt center.

- Cut 8 squares 2″ × 2″ for the half-square triangles.

- Cut 4 rectangles 1½″ × 2½″ for the Flying Geese.

- Cut 12 squares 1½″ × 1½″ for the block corners.

IVORY PRINTS

From each of 8 precut 10″ squares, cut 1 star set of:

- 1 square 2½″ × 2½″ for the star centers

- 2 squares 2″ × 2″ for the half-square triangles

- 4 squares 1½″ × 1½″ for the Flying Geese

Keep sets grouped together by print.

> ## tip
>
> Make a Christmas version of this versatile quilt with red and green prints and an embroidered wreath, or try a patriotic version with red and blue prints and an embroidered motif of your choice.

Making the Sawtooth Star Blocks

Use a ¼″ seam allowance. Follow the pressing arrows provided in the diagram(s). For more information about pressing seam allowances, see Pressing Matters (page 19).

FAUX FLYING GEESE UNITS

1. Use a pencil to lightly draw a diagonal line from corner to corner on the wrong side of 2 matching 2″ ivory squares.

2. Layer a marked ivory square atop a 2″ dark blue square, right sides together. Sew a scant ¼″ from each side of the drawn line. Repeat with a second marked ivory square and a 2″ light blue square. *fig. A*

3. Cut the pairs apart on the drawn line to make 4 half-square-triangles: 2 with dark blue and 2 with light blue triangles—all 4 with the same ivory print. Press open and trim to measure 1½″ × 1½″. *fig. B*

4. Repeat Steps 1–3 with the 7 remaining ivory star sets. *fig. C*

5. Sew a dark half-square triangle to a light half-square triangle, blue sides touching and ivory print on the top outside corners to make a faux Flying Geese unit. Dark blue will be to the left in 1 unit and to the right in the second unit. *fig. D*

6. Repeat Step 5 for all the matching ivory sets of half-square triangles. Keep the 2 faux Flying Geese units together with their original star set.

FLYING GEESE UNITS

Refer to the featured quilt to determine which 4 ivory star sets you plan to use for corner blocks and which 4 you plan to use for edge blocks.

1. Beginning with the *corner blocks*, use a pencil to lightly draw a diagonal line from corner to corner on the wrong side of a set of 4 ivory 1½″ squares.

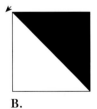

A.

B.

C. Half-square triangles

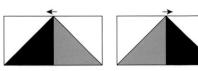

D. Faux Flying Geese units

2. Layer a marked square onto one end of a dark blue rectangle, as shown. Stitch the pair together on the drawn line. Trim the seam allowances to ¼˝. *fig. E*

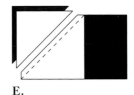

E.

3. In the same manner, stitch a second marked square to the opposite end of the rectangle. Trim the seam allowances to ¼˝. The complete Flying Geese unit measures 1½˝ × 2½˝. Make 2. *figs. F & G*

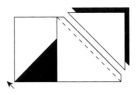

F.

4. Repeat Steps 1–3 for the 3 remaining ivory star sets chosen for the corner blocks. Make 4 sets.

5. Using the ivory star sets for the edge blocks, repeat Steps 1–4 for each set of 1½˝ squares, but this time make 1 dark-blue and 1 light-blue Flying Geese unit for each edge block. Make 4 sets. *fig. H*

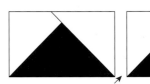

CORNER BLOCKS

Make sure that the same ivory print is used throughout to make 1 corner block.

1. Sew 1 dark-blue Flying Geese unit to the left of a 2½˝ ivory center square. Sew a faux Flying Geese unit to the right side of the center square, with the dark triangle on top, to make a center row.

2. Sew 2 dark blue 1½˝ corner squares to the ends of a dark-blue Flying Geese unit to make a top row.

3. Sew 1 dark blue 1½˝ corner square and 1 light blue 1½˝ corner square to the ends of the second faux Flying Geese unit, keeping the dark blues on one side and the light blues on the other, to make a bottom row.

4. Join the top and bottom rows to the center row to complete a corner block. Make 4 Sawtooth Star corner blocks from the remaining corner ivory star sets, each measuring 4½˝ × 4½˝. *fig. I*

EDGE BLOCKS

Make sure that the same ivory print is used throughout to make 1 edge block.

1. Sew a faux Flying Geese unit to the left and right sides of a 2½˝ ivory square, with the dark blue on top, to make a center row. Before sewing, re-press the seam allowances of the faux Flying Geese toward the light blue triangles.

2. Sew 2 dark blue 1½˝ squares to the ends of a dark-blue Flying Geese unit to make a top row.

3. Sew 2 light blue 1½˝ squares to the ends of a light-blue Flying Geese unit to make a bottom row.

4. Join the top and bottom rows to the center row to complete an edge block. Make 4 Sawtooth Star edge blocks from the remaining ivory prints, each measuring 4½˝ × 4½˝. *fig. J*

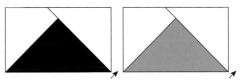

G. 2 Flying Geese units for corner blocks

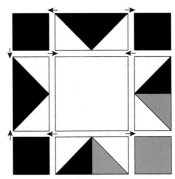

H. 2 Flying Geese units for edge blocks

I. Sawtooth Star corner block

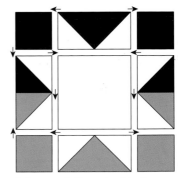

J. Sawtooth Star edge block

Assembling the Quilt

1. Join 2 Sawtooth Star edge blocks to opposite sides of the 4½˝ light-blue center square, facing the light blue edges to the inside to make the center row.

2. For the top row, join 2 Sawtooth Star corner blocks to opposite sides of a Sawtooth Star edge block, aligning the light blue sides to the bottom edge of the row. Press the seam allowances open.

3. Repeat Step 2 for the bottom row, but align the light blue sides of the blocks to the top edge of the row. Press the seam allowances open.

4. Join the top and bottom rows to the center row to complete the quilt center. Press the seam allowances open.

5. Sew a 12½˝ dark blue strip to the left and right sides of the quilt center.

6. Sew a 14½˝ dark blue strip to the top and bottom of the quilt center.

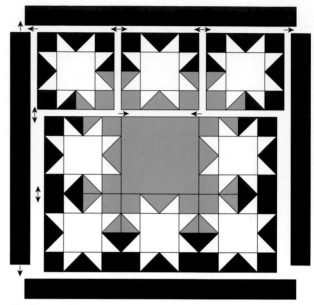

Quilt assembly

Embroidering the Quilt Center

Refer to Embroidery Basics (page 110) for detailed information.

1. Use a water-soluble fabric marking pen and the North Star Mini Quilt embroidery pattern (at right) to trace the snowflake on the quilt top as shown.

2. Layer and baste the quilt top and batting together.

3. Use 1 strand of *ivory perle cotton #12* to backstitch the snowflake through both layers.

Finishing the Quilt

1. Layer the embroidered quilt top and batting with the backing fabric. Baste.

2. Quilt as desired. The featured quilt shows *ivory* thread used to hand quilt an *X* in the center of each Sawtooth Star block.

3. Bind the quilt using the dark-blue binding strips. (Find additional information about binding a quilt at ctpub.com/quilting-sewing-tips.)

north star mini quilt
Embroidery Pattern

Snowflake

snowed in table runner

What could be better than being snowed in for a time in this cozy cabin in the woods as Shoo Fly "snowflakes" fall through a patchwork night sky?

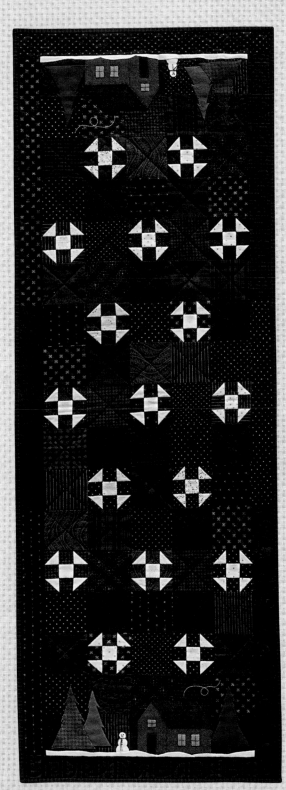

Machine quilted by Joyce Lundrigan

Materials

Cotton yardage is based on 40˝-wide fabric. Wool sizes are for felted wool. This pattern is scrap or precut friendly, though an entire precut pack or roll is not required. Precut sizes shown in the materials list indicate scrap sizes as well.

FABRIC

Dark blue prints: ⅓ yard for binding

   13 assorted precut 10˝ squares for background and blocks

   4 assorted fat eighths 9˝ × 22˝ for background and borders

White prints: 5–9 assorted squares for blocks, either precut 10˝ squares *or* scraps at least 8˝ × 8˝

Backing: 1¾ yards

FELTED WOOL

Brown: 6˝ × 10˝ for cabins

White: 6˝ × 10˝ for snow and snowmen

Assorted green: 3 squares 6˝ × 6˝ for trees

Textured dark brown: 6˝ × 6˝ for roofs

Dark brown: 3˝ × 3˝ for tree trunks

Red: 3˝ × 3˝ for doors and chimneys

Gold: 3˝ × 4˝ for windows

EMBROIDERY FLOSS

Colors to match wool

Black

Gray

Orange

OTHER SUPPLIES

Batting: 27˝ × 63˝

Freezer paper

Cutting

DARK BLUE PRINTS

From yardage, cut:

- 5 strips 2¼″ × width of fabric (WOF) for the binding

From each of 13 assorted precut 10″ squares, cut:

- 4 squares 3½″ × 3½″ for the background*

- 1 matching Shoo Fly background *set*** of:

  2 squares 2″ × 2″

  4 squares 1½″ × 1½″

From 1 fat eighth print, cut:

- 2 strips 2¼″ × 19″ for the border

- 4 squares 3½″ × 3½″ for the background*

- 1 Shoo Fly background set (See **, above.)

From 1 fat eighth print, cut:

- 2 strips 2¼″ × 15½″ for the border

- 4 squares 3½″ × 3½″ for the background*

- 1 Shoo Fly background set (See **, at left.)

From each of 2 fat eighth prints, cut:

- 2 strips 2¼″ × 18½″ for the border

- 4 squares 3½″ × 3½″ for the background*

- 1 Shoo Fly background set (See **, at left.)

*There will be a total of 68 background squares 3½″ × 3½″ and **17 Shoo Fly background sets.*

WHITE PRINTS

From 5–9 assorted precut 10″ squares, cut:

- 17 matching Shoo Fly *sets* of:

  2 squares 2″ × 2″

  1 square 1½″ × 1½″

Making the Appliquéd Panels

Use a ¼″ seam allowance. Follow the pressing arrows provided in the diagram(s). For more information about pressing seam allowances, see Pressing Matters (page 19).

BACKGROUND PANELS ASSEMBLY

1. Lay out 10 dark blue 3½″ squares in 2 rows of 5 squares each, as shown.

2. Join the squares into rows. Press the seam allowances open.

3. Join the rows and press the seam allowances open. This appliqué background panel should measure 15½″ × 6½″.

4. Repeat to make a second appliqué background panel.

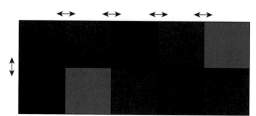

Appliqué background panel

APPLIQUÉ

Refer to Freezer-Paper Method (page 108) for step-by-step instructions. Refer to Stitching Wool Appliqués (page 109) as needed.

1. Use the Snowed In Table Runner appliqué patterns (pages 95–97) to prepare the wool appliqués.

2. Use the project photo as a guide to position the wool appliqués on the dark-blue pieced background panels.

Note: Certain appliqué pieces overlap, so you'll want to start by placing the background pieces—such as the tree trunks, cabins, and chimneys—first and then end with the uppermost appliqués, such as the strips of snow.

3. When you are satisfied with your arrangement on both panels, pin and whipstitch the wool appliqués in place with *1 strand* of embroidery floss that matches the wool. Make sure that the tips of the tree branches are at least ½˝ away from the raw edges of the appliqué panels and that the snow strips will be enclosed within the seams of the finished project. (It isn't necessary to whipstitch the bottoms of the snow strips.)

tip

For very sharp wool appliqué points, such as the tips of trees or tree branches, apply a dot of Fray Check to the very tip of the point after stitching the shape in place to help prevent fraying. Make sure to test the Fray Check on a scrap of same-color wool to ensure that it doesn't show after it dries.

EMBROIDERY

Refer to Embroidery Basics (page 110) for detailed information. Use *2 strands* of floss for all embroidery unless otherwise indicated.

1. Backstitch a vertical line to delineate the front and side faces of each cabin using *dark brown* floss. Use *1 strand* of the same floss to stitch long straight stitches horizontally and vertically over the windows to make panes.

2. Backstitch a curving line of smoke rising from each chimney using *gray* floss.

3. Backstitch a tiny mouth and stitch French knots for the eyes and buttons on each snowman using *black* floss.

4. Use *orange* floss to stitch a French knot for the nose on each snowman.

5. Use *3 strands* of *red* embroidery floss to make a scarf on each snowman by running the floss behind the snowman's neck and knotting the strands in front.

Making the Shoo Fly Blocks

1. Match 1 set of white Shoo Fly squares with 1 set of dark-blue Shoo Fly background squares.

2. Use a pencil to lightly draw a diagonal line from corner to corner on the wrong side of a matching pair of 2˝ white print squares.

3. Layer a 2˝ marked white square atop a 2˝ dark blue square, right sides together. Sew a scant ¼˝ from each side of the drawn line. *fig. A*

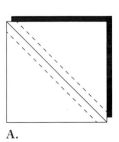

A.

4. Cut the unit apart on the drawn line to make 2 half-square triangles; press open. Trim the units to measure 1½″ × 1½″.

5. Repeat Steps 3 and 4 to make 4 matching half-square triangles. *fig. B*

6. Lay out 4 half-square triangles, 4 dark blue 1½″ squares, and 1 white 1½″ square in 3 rows of 3, as shown.

7. Join the pieces in each row.

8. Join the rows to complete a Shoo Fly block measuring 3½″ × 3½″.

9. Repeat Steps 1–8 to make a total of 17 Shoo Fly blocks. *fig. C*

B. Half-square triangle

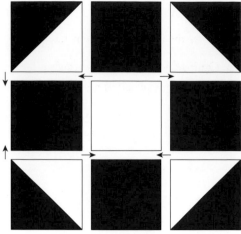

C. Shoo Fly block

Assembling the Table Runner

1. Join 5 assorted dark blue 3½″ squares into a row. Press the seam allowances open. Make 6 rows.

2. Join 3 dark blue 3½″ squares, alternating with 2 Shoo Fly blocks, to make a 2-block row. Press the seam allowances away from the Shoo Fly blocks. Repeat to make 4 rows.

3. Join 3 Shoo Fly blocks, alternating with 2 dark blue 3½″ squares, to make a 3-block row. Press the seam allowances away from the Shoo Fly blocks. Repeat to make 3 rows.

4. Lay out 2- and 3-block rows in alternating positions, with a row of dark blue squares between each. Join the 13 center rows. Press the seam allowances away from the Shoo Fly rows. The table runner center should measure 15½″ × 39½″.

5. Sew an appliquéd and embroidered panel to both short ends of the table runner center. Press the seam allowances away from the table runner center.

6. Sew an 18½″ border strip to opposite ends of a 15½″ border strip to make a pieced side border measuring 51½″. Press the seam allowances open. Repeat for a total of 2 pieced side borders.

7. Matching the centers, sew a pieced side border to the left and right sides of the table runner center.

8. Sew a 19″ dark-blue border strip to both ends of the table runner center.

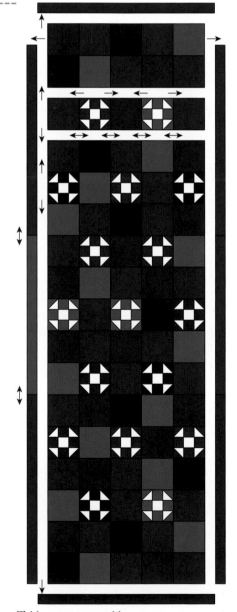

Table runner assembly

Finishing the Table Runner

1. Layer the appliquéd table runner top, batting, and backing. Baste.

2. Quilt as desired. The featured table runner was quilted with a crosshatch pattern in the center and swirls and stars in the appliqué panels. The outer border was quilted using the pattern Carousel Simply Swirl by Anne Bright Designs.

3. Bind the table runner using the dark-blue binding strips. (Find additional information about binding a quilt at ctpub.com/quilting-sewing-tips.)

---

snowed in table runner

Appliqué Patterns

Cut 2 of each except where noted. Optional: *For fusible web appliqué, reverse the patterns.*

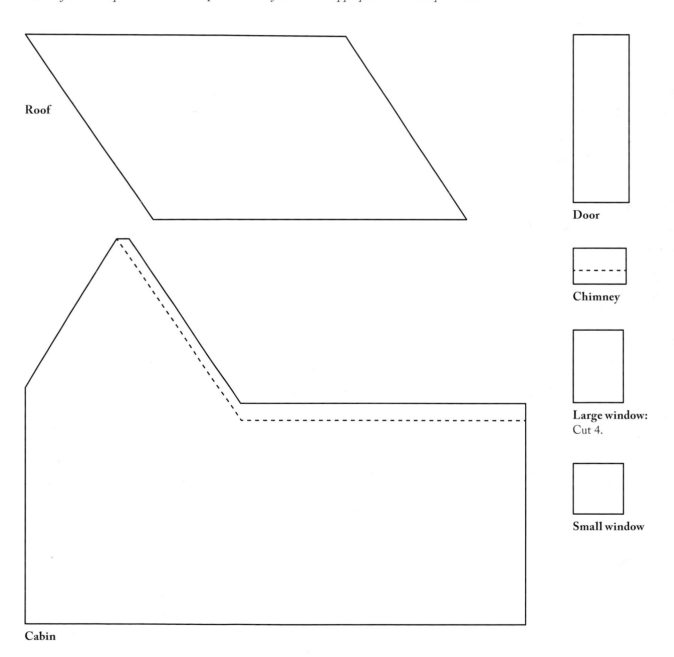

Roof

Door

Chimney

Large window:
Cut 4.

Small window

Cabin

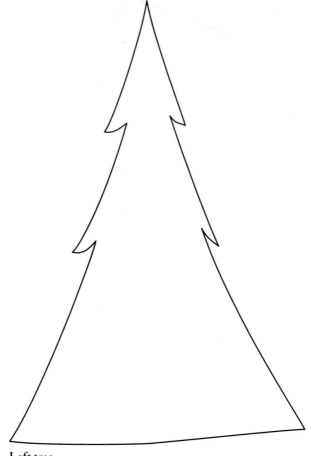

Tree trunk:
Cut 6.

Left tree

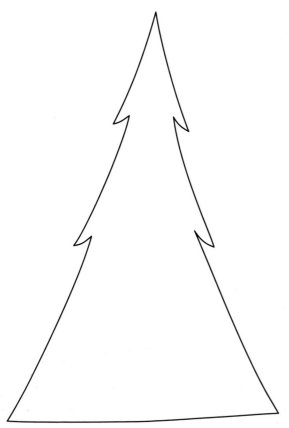

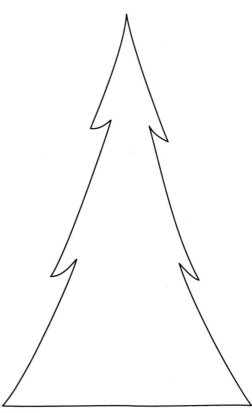

Right tree

Center tree

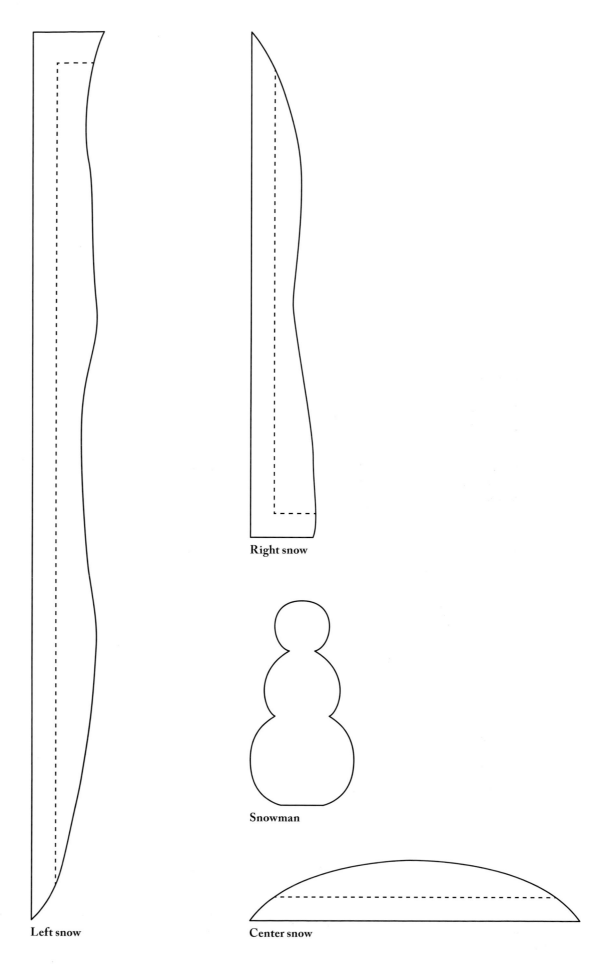

Left snow

Right snow

Snowman

Center snow

flurries quilt

Scrappy snowflakes gently drift atop a background of gray blue. This simple but striking quilt captures the magic of the moment when snow first begins to fall.

Machine quilted by
Joyce Lundrigan

Materials

Cotton yardage is based on 40˝-wide fabric. This pattern is scrap or precut friendly, though an entire precut pack or roll is not required. Precut sizes shown in the materials list indicate scrap sizes as well.

FABRICS

Medium blue print: 4¼ yards for blocks, background, and binding

Light blue print: ⅞ yard for Nine-Patch blocks

White prints*: 8 assorted fat eighths 9˝ × 22˝ for snowflake blocks

1 additional white-print precut 10˝ square

Backing: 4 yards

OTHER SUPPLIES

Batting: 72˝ × 72˝

*For a less scrappy version of this quilt, substitute 1 yard of a single white print.

Cutting

MEDIUM BLUE PRINT

- Cut 2 strips 14″ × width of fabric (WOF). Crosscut into:

  4 squares 14″ × 14″, cut in half diagonally twice to yield 16 setting triangles

  2 squares 7¼″ × 7¼″, cut in half diagonally once to yield 4 corner triangles

- Cut 21 strips 3½″ × WOF. Reserve 6 for the Nine-Patch blocks; then crosscut:

  9 strips into 11 squares 3½″ × 3½″ *per strip* for the snowflake blocks

  5 strips into 26 rectangles 1½″ × 3½″ *per strip* for the snowflake blocks

  1 strip into:

     1 additional square 3½″ × 3½″ for the snowflake blocks

     20 additional rectangles 1½″ × 3½″ for the snowflake blocks

- Cut 18 strips 1½″ × WOF. Crosscut 17 strips into:

  26 squares 1½″ × 1½″ *per strip* for the snowflake blocks

  Crosscut the remaining strip into:

  8 additional squares 1½″ × 1½″ for the snowflake blocks

- Cut 7 strips 2¼″ × WOF for the binding.

LIGHT BLUE PRINT

- Cut 8 strips 3½″ × WOF for the Nine-Patch blocks.

WHITE PRINTS

From each of the 8 assorted fat eighths, cut:

- 3 snowflake sets. 1 set includes:

  8 rectangles 1½″ × 3½″

  1 square 1½″ × 1½″

From an additional precut 10″ square, cut:

- 1 snowflake *set*

Keep snowflake sets together by print— 25 sets total.

Making the Nine-Patch Blocks

Use a ¼″ seam allowance. Follow the pressing arrows provided in the diagram(s). For more information about pressing seam allowances, see Pressing Matters (page 19).

1. Sew a 3½″ light blue strip to each long side of a 3½″ medium blue strip to make strip set A. Make 3 of strip set A.

2. Crosscut strip sets A into 32 units, each 3½″ wide. *fig. A*

3. Sew a 3½″ medium blue strip to each long side of a 3½″ light blue strip to make strip set B.

4. Cut 1 medium blue and 1 light blue 3½″ strip in half. Sew a medium blue half-strip to each long side of a light blue half-strip to make a short strip set B.

5. Crosscut strip sets B into 16 units total, each 3½″ wide. *fig. B*

6. Join 2 strip set A units to opposite sides of 1 strip set B unit to make a Nine-Patch block. Repeat to make 16 Nine-Patch blocks, each measuring 9½″ × 9½″. *fig. C*

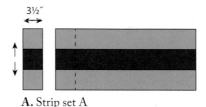

A. Strip set A

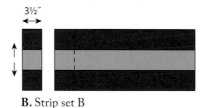

B. Strip set B

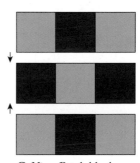

C. Nine-Patch block

Making the Snowflake Blocks

Select 1 snowflake *set* to work with until 1 block is complete.

SNOWFLAKE CENTER UNITS

1. Sew 1 medium blue 1½″ square to the left and right sides of 1 white 1½″ square to make a center row.

2. Sew 1 medium blue rectangle to the top and a second rectangle to the bottom of the center row. The snowflake center measures 3½″ × 3½″. *fig. A*

SNOWFLAKE SIDE UNITS

1. Use a pencil to lightly draw a diagonal line from corner to corner on the wrong side of 16 medium blue 1½″ squares.

2. Layer 1 marked square onto one end of a white rectangle with right sides together, as shown. Stitch the pair together along the drawn line. Pay close attention to the angle of the drawn line. Trim the seam allowances to ¼″. *fig. B*

3. Repeat Step 2 at the opposite end of the white rectangle. The angle of the drawn line should parallel the first stitching line. Stitch the pair together along the drawn line. Trim to form a half-chevron unit. Make 4 half-chevron units. *figs. C & D*

4. Repeat Steps 2 and 3, but this time create 4 half-chevron units that mirror the first 4 units. Note the changed angles of the parallel stitching lines. *fig. E*

5. Join 1 half-chevron and 1 mirrored half-chevron to opposite sides of a medium blue rectangle to make 1 snowflake side unit measuring 3½″ × 3½″. The orientation of the half-chevrons is crucial to success. Make 4 matching snowflake side units. *fig. F*

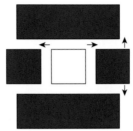

A. Snowflake center

B.

C.

D. Half-chevron

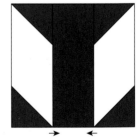

E. Mirrored half-chevron

F. Snowflake side unit

SNOWFLAKE BLOCK ASSEMBLY

1. Sew 1 snowflake side unit to the left and right sides of 1 snowflake center to make a center row. Pay attention to how the snowflake side units are oriented.

2. Sew 1 medium blue 3½″ square to the left and right sides of the remaining 2 snowflake units to make a top and a bottom row. The 2 rows are identical; the bottom row is turned 180° in the final block construction.

3. Join the top and bottom rows to the center row, following the orientation of the rows in the Snowflake block diagram. Press the seam allowances open.

4. Repeat all steps using *each* white snowflake *set* to create 1 Snowflake block for a total of 25, each measuring 9½″ × 9½″. *fig. G*

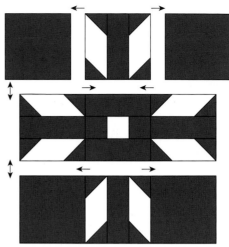

G. Snowflake block

Assembling the Quilt

1. Lay out the snowflake and Nine-Patch blocks in diagonal rows, alternating the blocks within rows and between rows as shown. Add the medium-blue setting triangles to each end of 8 rows.

2. Join the blocks and triangles in each row. Press the seam allowances away from the snowflake blocks.

3. Join the rows together; press the seam allowances open.

4. Sew a medium-blue corner triangle to each corner.

5. Trim and square up the quilt, making sure to leave a ¼″ seam allowance on all sides.

Quilt assembly

Finishing the Quilt

1. Layer the quilt top, batting, and backing. Baste.

2. Quilt as desired. The featured quilt was machine quilted using the edge-to-edge pattern Surf by Anne Bright Designs.

3. Bind the quilt using the medium-blue binding strips. (Find additional information about binding a quilt at ctpub.com/quilting-sewing-tips.)

jen's quiltmaking techniques

The following pages include my thoughts on various aspects of quilting, as well as some tips and techniques to help you successfully make the projects in this book. If you're new to quilting or if you'd like more detailed information about specific quiltmaking techniques, C&T Publishing has free resources online at ctpub.com/quilting-sewing-tips.

On Fabric

If I had to describe my quilting style, I'd call it "controlled scrappy." *Scrappy* because when it comes to fabric, I'm a firm believer that the more fabrics you use, the merrier. *Controlled* because I usually tend to work within a specific color palette rather than using every color in the rainbow, and because I often combine scrappy patchwork with only one or two background fabrics to keep a quilt from becoming too busy.

I love scrappy quilts because of the sparkle and interest that result from using a variety of prints and textures. I also love to see a favorite fabric repeated in my projects—that thread of continuity makes me feel connected to past quilters who had to employ a make-do approach to their quilting.

Scrap quilting sometimes requires more work up front to gather and prepare fabrics, and you can't always use timesaving methods for cutting and piecing. But for me, the finished product is worth it. When purchasing fabric, I tend to buy small cuts of a lot of different prints. My favorite cut is ⅓ yard. It's a bit more fabric than a fat quarter, and the extra length allows me to use it for borders or binding small projects.

Unless it is a precut, I always prewash my fabric. I wash similar colors together in cold water on a gentle cycle and toss in a dye-trapping sheet (such as a Shout Color Catcher) for good measure. Before I dry the fabric, I trim loose threads so they don't tangle in the dryer. I leave the fabric in the dryer until it is almost dry; then I remove it and spread it out flat, ready for ironing. Once pressed and folded, I sort and store the fabric by color and occasionally by type (for example, batiks, solids, and homespuns).

Once I've decided on the color palette for a quilt, I choose an assortment of small- and medium-scale prints in a variety of shades and values. When I can, I love to incorporate homespuns, ticking stripes, and even flannels in my projects; I love the texture and homey feel they impart. I tend to avoid large-scale prints in my quilts, but I do find them to be a great source of inspiration for color palettes.

Before I begin to quilt, I fan out the fabrics that I'm considering on the floor and stand back to get a sense for how they'll work together. It's amazing how a bit of distance can change your perspective. I pull out the fabrics that don't play well with others in terms of color or pattern and add additional fabrics as necessary. There isn't really a science behind my choices, and certainly there are no rules. It's more of an emotional response—if I like it, it stays, and if I don't, it goes!

On Finishing

I arrange to have most of my larger projects (lap quilts or bigger) and many of my mid-sized projects (table runners and wallhangings) professionally quilted by a longarm quilter. Professional quilting can beautifully enhance a quilt, and because I'm usually eager to move on to the next project, I love the quick turnaround time. But when I can, I still love to finish quilts by hand.

When I first started quilting, I hand quilted all of my quilts. My mom taught me how to hand quilt, and once I got used to the shockingly small needles, I was hooked! I love the authentic look of hand quilting, and the soft drape of the finished product is incomparable. My favorite tools for hand quilting are my lap hoop by The Grace Company, John James size 11 quilting needles, and YLI hand quilting thread (my favorite color is 003 Lt Brown).

I also love to finish some of my projects with big-stitch quilting. Big-stitch quilting is basically stitching a ⅛˝- to ¼˝-long running stitch through the quilt layers. This easy type of stitching moves along faster than regular hand quilting, and because it's more visible than hand quilting, it can do double duty as an added design element—especially if you use a complementary color thread. When I big-stitch quilt, I like to use perle cotton #8 or #12, and because of its heavier weight, I use an embroidery needle (size 5).

Occasionally, I do machine quilt projects at home. Because I'm working on a standard sewing machine, I typically only machine quilt smaller projects with straight or gently curving lines. I like to use a walking foot, and I try to use thread that will blend into the background. I keep my machine quilting simple by stitching-in-the-ditch and stitching alongside seams or by echo quilting appliquéd elements. If I machine quilt a crosshatch or straight lines to add texture, I use narrow masking tape to mark the lines for quilting.

A quick word about basting: When I'm hand or big-stitch quilting a project, I tend to thread baste the layers together. But with a very small project (such as a mini quilt) or when I'm machine quilting, I prefer to use a combination of spray basting adhesive such as 505 Spray and Fix and straight pins or safety pins. The spray basting adhesive does a wonderful job of holding the layers together, and the pins provide a bit of extra insurance that the layers won't shift during quilting.

ADDING A HANGING SLEEVE TO A SMALL QUILT

1. Cut a strip of fabric 5˝ wide × the width of the quilt.

2. Fold the short ends of the strip toward the wrong side of the fabric ⅜˝ twice. Press.

3. Sew ¼˝ from the folded edges to create hems. *fig. A*

4. Fold the strip in half lengthwise with the wrong sides together and press to form a sleeve. *fig. B*

5. On the back of the quilt, align the raw edges of the sleeve even with the top edge of the trimmed quilt and center it along this edge. Baste the sleeve to the quilt ⅛˝ from the raw edges.

6. Bind the quilt. When the binding is sewn to the quilt, the raw edges of the sleeve will be enclosed inside the binding.

7. Hand sew the bottom edge of the sleeve to the quilt, stitching through the backing and batting.

SINGLE-FOLD BINDING

I bind small projects like the Little House quilts with single-fold binding. Small quilts typically don't experience enough wear and tear to merit a double-fold binding, and single-fold binding reduces bulk and saves fabric. Typically I'll use 1¼˝ strips for a single-fold binding. (Find additional information about binding a quilt at ctpub.com/quilting-sewing-tips.)

1. Join the 1¼˝-wide binding strips together on the diagonal to form a single length of binding. Press these seams open to reduce bulk. Do not fold the strip in half lengthwise.

2. Sew the binding to the front of the layered and squared-up quilt top with right sides together.

3. With the quilt top facing down, the binding extending away from the quilt, and beginning along the center of one edge of the quilt, fold the raw edge of the binding toward the wrong side so it meets the edge of the quilt. Finger-press.

4. Fold the binding over a second time to overlap the quilt edge, making sure that the folded edge of the binding covers the line of stitching. Pin or clip the binding to hold it in place.

5. Continue folding and securing the binding around the outside of the quilt, mitering the corners as you go.

6. Hand stitch the binding to the back of the quilt using a blind stitch and 1 strand of matching hand-quilting thread.

⅜˝

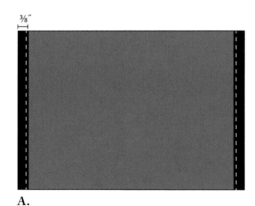

A.

B.

Paper-Piecing Basics

Paper piecing, or *foundation piecing*, is a method for making quilt blocks by sewing pieces of fabric to a paper foundation pattern in numerical order. It's a wonderful technique to use for sharp, accurate points; complicated shapes; or odd measurements. I especially love paper piecing because of its flexibility. Once you have a foundation pattern, it's simple to enlarge or reduce it to make the exact-size blocks you need to fit into any project. For that reason, it's my favorite way to piece miniature quilt blocks. Paper piecing uses a bit more fabric, but you don't have to worry about precise cutting or fabric grainlines. Once you get the hang of it, it's fast and fun!

HOW TO PAPER PIECE

1. Photocopy or download and print the pattern onto foundation paper. (For information about downloadable pdfs, see Foundation Paper-Piecing Patterns, page 10.) Note that, just as in standard piecing, paper-pieced quilt blocks may be made up of multiple components. On a typical foundation pattern, the solid lines are sewing lines. The solid perimeter line represents the edges of the finished block, and the outermost dashed or dotted line is the line on which you trim your block, allowing for a ¼″ seam allowance. The number within each area is the sequence in which each area is covered; the letters correlate to a fabric selection guide in the instructions so you know which fabric to place. *fig. C*

2. Trim each pattern ¼″ outside the dashed/dotted line, being sure to keep the foundation pattern intact.

3. Place the foundation pattern right side down on a flat surface. Position fabric 1 right side up over the marked area 1. Hold the foundation pattern and fabric up to a light source to make sure that the fabric fully covers area 1 and that it extends at least ¼″ beyond the lines on all sides of the shape. When you are satisfied with its position, pin the fabric in place. *fig. D*

4. Layer fabric 2 onto fabric 1 with right sides together, aligning the edges parallel to the sewing line between areas 1 and 2 and extending at least ¼″ into area 2. Once again, hold your work up to a light to confirm that when fabric 2 is flipped open after sewing, it will completely cover area 2 *and* extend ¼″ beyond all edges of area 2. You can test this by pinning the 2 fabrics together on the sewing line and flipping fabric 2 open. If the fabric does not fully cover area 2 including the ¼″ seam allowances, reposition the fabric. Once you're satisfied with its position, pin the fabric to hold it in place. With the foundation pattern right side up, stitch on the sewing line between areas 1 and 2 using a shortened stitch length (18–20 stitches per inch). Be sure to start and stop sewing a few stitches beyond the sewing line to help prevent the seams from pulling apart when you remove the paper. *fig. E*

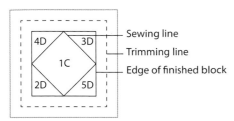

C. Foundation pattern

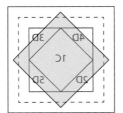

D. Wrong side of pattern up

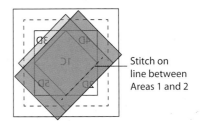

E. Position fabric 2 over fabric 1 with right sides together.

5. After stitching, reconfirm that fabric 2 fully covers area 2 and extends ¼″ beyond area 2 on all sides. Then fold the foundation pattern back at the stitching line and trim the excess fabric only (Do not cut the paper!), leaving a scant ¼″ seam allowance. Press with a dry iron to set the seam; then flip fabric 2 open and press again. *figs. F & G*

6. In the same manner, continue positioning and stitching the fabric pieces in place in numerical order until all areas have been covered. *figs. H–J*

7. Once all the areas have been covered, use a rotary cutter and ruler to trim the block through all layers along the outermost dashed line. *fig. K*

8. Gently remove the foundation paper from the back of the finished block. If necessary, use tweezers to get into tiny corners. You might want to wait to remove the paper from the blocks until after you've sewn them to another block (or patch, sashing strip, and so on). This helps you accurately sew blocks together because you can stitch along the sewing lines.

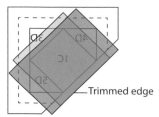

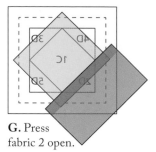

F. Trim seam allowances to ¼″.

G. Press fabric 2 open.

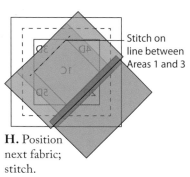

H. Position next fabric; stitch.

Stitch on line between Areas 1 and 3

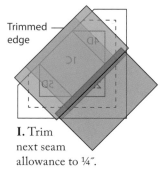

Trimmed edge

I. Trim next seam allowance to ¼″.

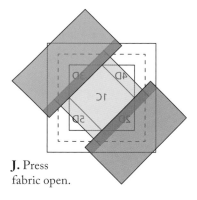

J. Press fabric open.

K. Trimmed block (including seam allowances)

PAPER-PIECING TIPS

- Foundation paper specifically designed for paper piecing is readily available online or in quilt shops. It's lightweight and easy to remove from your finished blocks yet strong enough to run through a printer or photocopier. If you decide to use regular copy paper—and I've been known to do so—be very careful when removing it to avoid pulling out stitches.

- If the foundation pattern you are using is printed only in black and white, consider coloring the areas with colored pencils to avoid confusion when placing fabrics.

- When paper piecing, remember that the finished unit will be a mirror image of the printed pattern.

- When positioning fabric pieces prior to sewing, it helps to hold the foundation pattern and fabric up to a light source such as a window, lamp, or lightbox to check your placement.

- Shorten your stitch length to 18–20 stitches per inch. This helps to perforate the foundation paper more and makes removing the paper easier.

- Start and stop sewing a few stitches beyond each sewing line.

- When pressing during piecing, do not use steam because it can distort the foundation paper.

Wool Appliqué Basics

I love to embellish my quilts with wool appliqué because of the texture, dimension, and color it adds. Felted wool is a dream to work with because it resists fraying and you don't need to turn the edges under when appliquéing it.

FELTING WOOL

Beautifully dyed felted wool is readily available online and at quilt shops, but it's also easy to felt your own wool.

1. Make sure to use 100% wool.

2. Wool can shrink substantially during felting. The pattern measurements in this book are for pre-felted wool, so if you plan to felt your own wool, buy extra to allow for shrinkage.

3. Wash the wool in a washing machine using hot water and a small amount of laundry soap. The dye from wool can run, so be sure to wash like colors together. I often add a couple pairs of jeans to the washing machine when I'm washing wool to increase the agitation.

4. Dry the washed wool in a clothes dryer on high heat until it is almost dry. Then remove the wool and lay it flat to finish drying. Press as necessary.

> ### tip
>
> Very small pieces of wool can also be felted by agitating them by hand in a sink of hot, soapy water. The more you manipulate the wool, the denser the fibers will become. Rinse the wool in cool water and position it flat to dry.

PREPARING WOOL APPLIQUÉS

I use two application methods for wool appliqué—freezer paper and fusible web. I tend to use the freezer-paper method most often because the wool shapes remain repositionable. With the freezer-paper method, there is also no need to worry about reversing patterns and the wool doesn't lose any of its loft during pressing. It's also great for large shapes.

While the freezer-paper method is my preferred technique, at times the fusible web method is invaluable. I use the fusible web method for applying small shapes that I don't want to shift or when I'm concerned about sharp points or thin shapes fraying. I also like to use fusible web when I want to fix a lot of shapes in place at once for a portable stitching project.

Freezer-Paper Method

1. Trace the appliqué shapes onto the dull side of freezer paper, leaving at least ½″ between shapes.

2. Cut out each drawn shape roughly ¼″ outside the drawn lines. *fig. L*

3. With the shiny or waxed side down, iron the freezer-paper pattern onto the right side of the felted wool (there may not be a right side) using a dry iron on the wool setting.

4. Cut out each shape through all layers along the drawn lines. Remove the freezer paper. *fig. M*

5. Position the shapes as desired on the background and pin them in place to secure them for stitching.

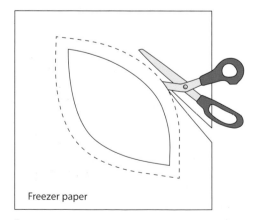

Freezer paper

L.

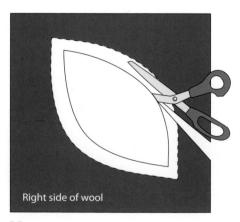

Right side of wool

M.

Fusible Web Method

1. Trace the appliqué shapes onto the paper side of lightweight paper-backed fusible web (I use HeatnBond Lite), leaving at least ½˝ between shapes. When using this method, note that asymmetrical shapes should be reversed before tracing.

2. Cut out each drawn shape roughly ¼˝ outside the drawn lines. *fig. N*

3. Following the manufacturer's instructions, iron the fusible web pattern, glue side down, onto the wrong side of the felted wool (there may not be a wrong side).

4. Cut out each shape through all the layers along the drawn lines. Remove the paper backing. *fig. O*

5. Position the wool shapes as desired on the background, and fuse them in place using a hot, dry iron. Because of the thickness of the wool, it can take quite a bit of heat to activate the adhesive. I often use a pressing cloth during this step to ensure that the wool does not scorch.

6. After the shapes are pressed in place, flip your work over and press again from the wrong side to make sure that the shapes are fully adhered to the background.

STITCHING WOOL APPLIQUÉS

The whipstitch is my favorite stitch to use for wool appliqué. It is fast, easy, and casual in appearance. Occasionally I use a blanket stitch to appliqué wool if I want a more formal look or if I want the stitching to be more visible.

My preferred thread for wool appliqué is a single strand of embroidery floss because it's inexpensive and readily available in a rainbow of colors. I also like to use perle cotton #8 or #12 from time to time for a different effect. Most of the time, I match the color of the appliqué thread to the wool, but sometimes I use a contrasting color if I want the stitching to stand out as an additional or unifying design element.

Stitch wool appliqués with an embroidery needle (size 5) and an 18˝-long strand of floss. Make stitches ⅛˝–¼˝ long, approximately the same distance apart, and perpendicular to the edge of the wool shape. See Stitches (page 110) for detailed diagrams of the whipstitch, the blanket stitch, and other decorative embroidery stitches.

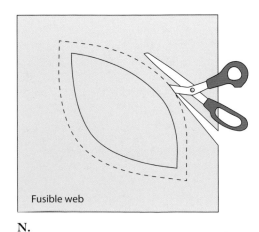

Fusible web

N.

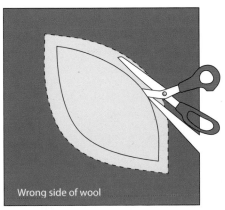

Wrong side of wool

O.

Embroidery Basics

Simple embroidery is another of my favorite ways to embellish quilted projects.

PREPARING FOR STITCHING

• Use a lightbox to help transfer an embroidery pattern to the stitching background.

• A water-soluble fabric marking pen makes it easy to mark work for embroidery. Remember to test the pen on a scrap of fabric before marking to be sure that the marking will come out once you are finished stitching. Never use an iron on fabric that is marked with a water-soluble marking pen until the ink is removed—it may set the ink. To remove the ink, lightly spritz the marks with water, blot the marks dry with a tea towel, and allow the fabric to dry flat. Repeat as necessary to fully remove the ink.

• Layering a quilt or background fabric with batting prior to embroidering adds extra dimension to the stitching and prevents the thread ends from showing through. Use spray basting adhesive between the layers to hold the quilt top and batting together before embroidering.

STITCHING

• Use an embroidery hoop to hold your work still while stitching. A 4˝- to 5˝-diameter hoop is suitable for most projects, but when the quilt top or background is layered with batting, a larger hoop may be necessary.

• Choose an embroidery needle based on the thickness of the thread that you're using. You should try to use the finest needle that you can without having to struggle to pull the thread through the fabric. The larger the size number, the finer the needle. A size 5 needle works well for perle cotton #8 or #12, but a smaller needle will work for 1 or 2 strands of embroidery floss.

• My thread of choice is 6-strand embroidery floss. I use 2 strands of floss for most stitching, but 3 or more strands for French knots.

STITCHES

Backstitch

Blanket stitch

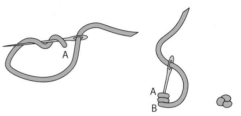

French knot

Lazy daisy

Running stitch

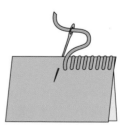

Whipstitch

about the author

Jen Daly has been sewing and crafting all her life, but she didn't make her first *real* quilt until 2003. Busy with 3 young kids at home, she was searching for a creative outlet for her evenings and thought that quilting might fit the bill. Jen decided to make a Bowtie quilt and intended to do all the work by hand, but when it took 3 nights to complete the first block, she decided to switch to machine piecing. By the time she had pieced and hand quilted the 64-block quilt, Jen was hooked!

After making several more quilts, Jen decided to try her hand at design. In 2010, *Quilters Newsletter* published an article she wrote describing her experience as an entrant of the Keepsake Quilting Challenge, and in 2011, her first design was published as a companion project for a second quilting article. Since then, Jen's designs have been published in numerous magazines and calendars. She is also a quilting teacher and a regular contributor to the Moda Bake Shop.

Jen loves to make scrappy quilts, combining different fabrics such as homespuns and flannels with quilting cottons. She also loves handwork and frequently adds wool appliqué and simple embroidery to her projects to provide both personality and texture. Jen most often works with traditional fabrics and color palettes, but she also has a contemporary side that she indulges occasionally by experimenting with modern fabrics and colors.

Jen lives with her family in New Hampshire, where she is continually inspired by the beautiful and ever-changing landscape.

Follow Jen on social media!

Website: jendalyquilts.com

Facebook: /jendalyquilts

Instagram: @jendalyquilts

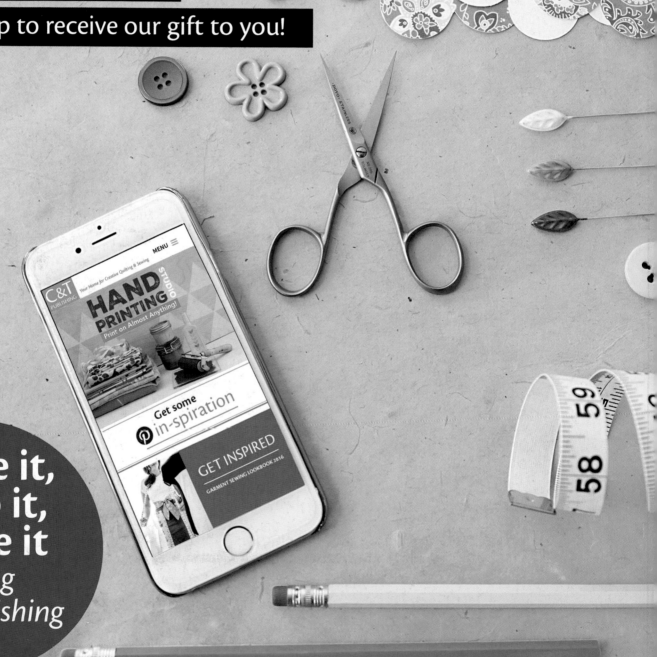